"Fernandez and Allison have provided a much needed practical guide for those desiring to pursue a doctorate in education specifically. Current practitioners considering pursuing the terminal degree will particularly find this work extremely helpful. The *Travel Journal* and *Packing Checklist* sections in each chapter are a creative way to provide students with the needed motivation on their journey to degree completion."

Dr. Michael Rosato, Professor and Dean, School of Education, Howard Payne University, USA

"A thorough, sincere, and out-of-the-box testament of what a doctoral journey means for all who decide to undertake it. Filled with excerpts of those who have *been there and done that*, Drs. Fernandez and Allison have brought forth one of the most straightforward accounts of what it takes to succeed in the doctoral academic world."

Dr. Pablo G. Siboldi, Assistant Principal, Aldine Independent School District, USA

Navigating the Doctorate in Education

Navigating the Doctorate in Education is an engaging and honest conversation for anyone considering pursuing a doctorate degree in education. This book helps prospective students navigate the journey from choosing the right university to completing the research and achieving the ultimate title of doctor of education. Success in this advanced degree journey depends on understanding where to go; financial, personal, and professional demands; and the educational expectations of a doctorate degree. There are nuances of the process, whether you take classes on campus or online, that every candidate should know before beginning this terminal degree. A timely text, *Navigating the Doctorate in Education* encapsulates perspectives from professors and former doctoral candidates so you will be informed and prepared for success.

Julie Fernandez is Dean of the College of Education at Charleston Southern University, USA.

Krista Allison is Program Chair of the EdD program at Charleston Southern University, USA.

Navigating the Doctorate in Education

Planning Your Journey

Julie Fernandez
and Krista Allison

Routledge
Taylor & Francis Group
NEW YORK AND LONDON

Designed cover image: © Getty Images

First published 2024
by Routledge
605 Third Avenue, New York, NY 10158

and by Routledge
4 Park Square, Milton Park, Abingdon, Oxon, OX14 4RN

Routledge is an imprint of the Taylor & Francis Group, an informa business

© 2024 Julie Fernandez and Krista Allison

The right of Julie Fernandez and Krista Allison to be identified as authors of this work has been asserted in accordance with sections 77 and 78 of the Copyright, Designs and Patents Act 1988.

All rights reserved. No part of this book may be reprinted or reproduced or utilised in any form or by any electronic, mechanical, or other means, now known or hereafter invented, including photocopying and recording, or in any information storage or retrieval system, without permission in writing from the publishers.

Trademark notice: Product or corporate names may be trademarks or registered trademarks, and are used only for identification and explanation without intent to infringe.

Library of Congress Cataloging-in-Publication Data
Names: Fernandez, Julie, author. | Allison, Krista, author.
Title: Navigating the doctorate in education : planning your journey / Julie Fernandez and Krista Allison.
Description: New York : Routledge, 2024. | Includes bibliographical references and index.
Identifiers: LCCN 2023041333 | ISBN 9781032597928 (hbk) | ISBN 9781032596006 (pbk) | ISBN 9781003456278 (ebk)
Subjects: LCSH: Doctor of education degree—United States. | Universities and colleges—United States—Graduate work. | Dissertations, Academic—United States. | Education—Research—Methodology.
Classification: LCC LB1742 .F47 2024 | DDC 378.20973—dc23/eng/20230925
LC record available at https://lccn.loc.gov/2023041333

ISBN: 978-1-032-59792-8 (hbk)
ISBN: 978-1-032-59600-6 (pbk)
ISBN: 978-1-003-45627-8 (ebk)

DOI: 10.4324/9781003456278

Typeset in Perpetua
by Apex CoVantage, LLC

Contents

Preface — xii

PART I
Planning Where You Want to Go — 1

1 Introduction to Education Doctoral Programs — 3
   Introduction 3
   EdS, EdD, and PhD—What Is the Difference? 6
   Financial Commitment 11
   Summary 12

2 Which Program Fits My Professional Goals? — 14
   Introduction 14
   University Options 14
   Campus-Based 16
   Online 19
   Program Quality and Support 21
   Cohort Systems 23
   Transfer Credits 23
   Summary 24

PART II
Packing Your Skills Suitcase — 27

3 Assessing Your Skills — 29
   Introduction 29
   Adult Learning Theory 30
      Learners Need to Know Why, What, and How 30

CONTENTS

      Self-Concept of the Learner   32
      Prior Experience of the Learner   32
      Readiness to Learn   33
      Orientation to Learning   34
      Motivation to Learn   34
   Learning Styles   35
   Self-Efficacy   37
   Organizational Skills   39
   Academic/Scholarly Writing   40
   Reading Skills   42
   Statistics   43
   Accommodations   44
   Summary   44

4 Preparing Yourself for the Road Ahead   **47**
   Introduction   47
   Time Management   50
   Work Area and Supplies   53
   Self-Care   54
   Summary   56

PART III
Avoiding Quicksand on the Trail   57

5 The Big Three: Classes, Comprehensive Exams, and Capstone Projects   **59**
   Introduction   59
   Number 1: Classes and Assignments   59
      Planning Your Writing Assignments   61
   Number 2: Comprehensive Exams   62
   Number 3: Capstone Projects   62
      Dissertation in Practice (DiP)   63
      Traditional Dissertation   63
   Summary   65

6 Rules of the Road   **67**
   Introduction   67
   Syllabus   68
   Attendance   68
   Late Assignments   69
   Tuition   69
   Continuous Enrollment   70

Complaints about Faculty   *70*
Plagiarism   *71*
Artificial Intelligence (AI)   *72*
Academic Integrity Violations and Appeals   *72*
Summary   *73*

PART IV
Crossing the Oceans   75

7 Research Expedition   77
Introduction   *77*
Choosing a Topic   *77*
Narrowing the Topic   *79*
Additional Considerations as You Explore the Topic   *80*
What Is Bias Research?   *80*
Consider Your Intentions   *82*
Begin with the End in Mind   *82*
Saving the World   *82*
Summary   *83*

8 Your Tour Guides   85
Introduction   *85*
Faculty in the Program   *85*
Your Chairperson and Committee   *86*
How to Pick a Chairperson   *87*
How to Pick Committee Members   *88*
Worst-Case Scenarios Do Happen   *88*
Lessons in Humility   *91*
Summary   *92*

9 The Voyage   94
Introduction   *94*
Alignment in Research   *94*
Abstract   *95*
Chapter 1: Introduction   *95*
Chapter 2: Literature Review   *98*
   Finding Research for Literature Reviews   *99*
   References vs. Bibliography   *99*
   Organizing Your Research Articles   *100*
Chapter 3: Methodology   *100*
   Qualitative, Quantitative, or Mixed Methods?   *100*
   Collecting Data   *102*

CONTENTS

    Chapter 4: Results   *104*
    Chapter 5: Conclusions and Discussion of the Results   *105*
       Writing Suggestions for Chapter 5   *106*
    Remember to Breathe, But Also Keep Writing!   *108*
    Pace Your Progress   *108*
    Summary   *108*

10 Documenting Your Journey   **110**
    Introduction   *110*
    Presentation Basics   *110*
    Preproposal/Candidacy Defense   *111*
    Deadlines and Time Frames   *111*
    Proposal Defense   *112*
    Dissertation Defense   *112*
    Summary   *113*

11 The Final Defense   **114**
    Introduction   *114*
    Final Defense   *114*
    Final Defense Checklist   *115*
    After the Final Defense   *116*
    Electronic Submissions   *116*
    Summary   *117*

PART V
Planning Your Next Adventure   **119**

12 Career: School Leadership   **121**
    Introduction   *121*
    Mapping Out Your Future   *122*
    School District Leadership Positions   *122*
       Superintendent   *122*
    District-Level Leadership   *124*
    Campus Principal   *125*
    Education Consultant   *127*
    Summary   *128*

13 Career Path: Higher Education   **130**
    Introduction   *130*
    Credentials   *131*
    Understanding the Landscape   *132*

Tenure-Track *133*
Non-Tenure-Track *135*
Faculty Rank *135*
Adjuncts *136*
Lecturers/Instructors *137*
Visiting Faculty *137*
Assistant Professor *137*
Associate Professor *138*
Full Professor *138*
Professor Emeritus *139*
Finding a Job at a Higher Education Institution *139*
   The Search *139*
   The Application *140*
   The Interviews *140*
   Curriculum Vitae vs. Résumé *141*
Summary *142*

Bon Voyage 144
Index 145

Preface

Welcome aboard! This book is intended to allow prospective doctorate students to learn the ins and outs of programs in the United States. Not every program is the same, and some information shared may or may not apply to your chosen university. The assumption is that you will now be equipped to ask questions before accepting this upper-level degree challenge.

We have been working with hundreds of doctoral students as faculty, teaching courses in person and online, chairing dissertation committees, and serving as committee members. Our experiences, both positive and negative, were our motivation for writing this book. So many students come into these programs unprepared for the educational work they must do. They come unprepared for the sacrifices of time, money, and relationships. Some students have this attitude that they are consumers of the degree and not producers of research. This degree is about being independent learners striving to understand their profession and become scholars in the search for solutions. We are encouraged that many students seeking this degree are outstanding and produce work that could change our world. This book must encourage more professionals to seek this degree, but with eyes wide open. Knowledge is powerful and can relieve the stress of the unknown.

The book is arranged into sections based on the notion that attaining a doctoral degree is a journey. Just as one may buy a map before taking a journey, Section I allows you to create a plan for where you would like to go and equips you with some ideas to keep in mind as you consider the EdD journey. Section II assists you in assessing and preparing for the trip ahead. Skills and self-assessment are an important part of this journey, and we want to equip you for the road ahead. The next portion of the book, Section III, is designed to highlight some of the challenges one may face on the journey to a doctoral degree. With practical advice and shared testimonials from those who have traveled the road before, we hope to help you avoid any quicksand. Section IV details the research expedition and dissertation experience, allowing you to gain an understanding of the process

PREFACE

before diving into the open waters of the EdD. Finally, Section V concludes with some valuable information for planning the next adventure and life after the EdD has been obtained.

Each chapter of the book is designed with snapshots, travel journal prompts, and a packing checklist to document your travels. Snapshots are short vignettes of travelers who have gone before. Sometimes, it helps to hear the experiences of others and learn from those who have successfully completed a doctoral degree, so we have included the voices of many graduates to better equip you. A good travel journal is another way to document your travels. Each chapter of this book is designed with travel journal prompts to assist you in reflecting on your values, ideas, and goals. Additionally, each chapter includes a packing checklist so that nothing is forgotten. A good checklist will ensure the journey goes smoothly and all necessary items are packed and ready for the adventure. Our packing checklists at the end of each chapter are designed with this notion in mind and will prepare you for the doctoral journey ahead. We hope the snapshots, travel journal prompts, and packing checklists help as you embark on your journey.

This degree is a journey of self-discovery. You will be testing your endurance, time management, and worldview. When you reach your final destination—earning the degree—the overwhelming sense of accomplishment brings most tears of joy. We hope this book helps map out this journey. Happy travels!

xiii

Part I
Planning Where You Want to Go

Chapter 1

Introduction to Education Doctoral Programs

CHAPTER OBJECTIVES

- Determine which doctorate is appropriate for your career pathway.
- Select the university program that aligns with your professional goals and learning style.
- Plan your strategies for the financial challenges of this degree.
- Reflect on your motivations for seeking a doctoral degree.

INTRODUCTION

The idea of getting a doctoral degree is keeping you up at night. This wild idea of doing something unique yet terrifying is nagging your thoughts and may even come from trusted friends or supervisors. They see potential in you that you may need to see or recognize. You may even have people discourage you from taking this journey. Why spend the money and time when you could do something else? Do you want to go back to college? Ignore the naysayers and consider the possibilities of achieving something that most people would be too afraid to attempt. If you believe this is right for you, let nothing stop you from exploring the possibilities.

As you begin this journey, you begin researching programs at universities. Doctoral programs are different and, at the same time, follow a tradition of higher education that is hundreds of years in the making. Let us imagine this process as a very different process that has been practiced for hundreds of years: making bread. First, grains are chosen and harvested from the field. Your grains represent your research phase as you identify potential programs and universities. Some policies and procedures may seem archaic, but the system was created to weed out the wheat from the chaff. Understanding the rules of good and bad is the next step as one prepares the wheat to become bread. Chaff is inedible for humans, so it must be separated from the seed we can consume. Every university

DOI: 10.4324/9781003456278-2   **3** manages its doctoral education programs differently. While this book is intended to give insight into the process and procedures common to most universities, it is expected to cover something other than university-specific attributes. Institutions may have different policies, just as you may have different ingredients in the bread. You must review the university's graduate policies and catalog for the program or university-specific rules. Differing loaves of bread fulfill different dietary needs; different programs fulfill the needs of diverse student populations.

This book will allow you to reflect on whether this journey is right for you and give you a basis to ask questions of the faculty and leadership at your university of choice. Sticking with the notion of bread, I remember craving a croissant when I was pregnant. Nothing and no one would stop me from devouring the croissant from the pastry shop down the street! Similarly, if achieving a doctoral degree is in your head and heart, do not allow anything to stop you.

It is best to go into this endeavor with eyes wide open and understanding the expectations associated with this degree. Many pieces to the doctoral program journey should be more intuitive. Everyone who starts a doctoral education program has good intentions to finish strong. However, many need help to do so. This statement is not written to discourage you from considering this direction in your career but a conversation about the challenges you will face. After working with hundreds of doctoral students at three universities, I have seen much, heard much, and experienced the ups and downs of my doctoral students. Nothing is worse than having students fail or drop out of the program because they were unaware of the expectations.

If you still feel the call to seek the highest degree of education offered, it is time to take a deep breath and step onto the pathway for this long and challenging journey. The trail might be bumpy with twists and turns, rocky inclines, and steep learning curves, but the destination of walking the stage, getting a hood and diploma, and being called "Doctor" is worth every blister.

MY STORY

What was I thinking? This question is in every doctoral student's mind at one time or another during their journey. The programs are intended to stretch your thought process and change your worldview. It is also just exhausting. I have had that experience and have heard hundreds of doctoral students express these feelings at different stages of the process. I have consoled many students as they wonder if the money, time, and tears are worth the effort so they can be called "Doctor." Yes, it is worth it. My journey was a series of starts and stops. I began my higher education graduate experience a few years into my teaching career. I need to learn more about teaching reading to be the best reading teacher.

I entered an MS degree to become a reading specialist. I connected with my professors, and they saw potential and became my mentors. After I completed the program, they asked me to be an adjunct instructor for undergraduate students. I loved teaching these preservice teachers. A few years later, I was called to my principal's office and was told that the university wanted to hire me for a year as a "teacher in residence." The district agreed to give me a year's leave to teach at the university. It was one of the best experiences of my life. I enjoyed interacting with the young adults and learning more about the topics I taught. I believe I became a stronger teacher in public schools because of this experience.

I took advantage of the faculty discount for courses and began my post-graduate studies in school administration. After that fantastic year, the university offered me the director of student teaching position. What a dilemma: I loved higher education, but I still wasn't ready to leave public schools. Instead, I accepted an assistant principal's job and later became a principal. It was a good choice, because the school leadership positions expanded my knowledge of schools and children. The seed had been planted, though. I knew teaching in higher education was something I wanted to do when the time was right. My university mentors encouraged me to get a doctorate if I planned to teach at the college level.

It was a start-and-stop process. I walked onto a big university campus in Houston, determined to apply for the doctoral degree program, but nerves overtook me, and I chickened out. I sat in a campus burger joint and created a list of why I was not doctoral student material. Was I smart enough? Could I manage my young family and job while going to school? How would I preserve my marriage through stressful times? Can I still maintain all the demands of my job? Where is the money going to come from? I drove home discouraged and feeling like a loser.

A couple of years later, I decided to apply to another state university with an excellent reputation for its program. I applied and was asked to come in for an interview. My GRE scores were not off the charts but within the requirements, and my graduate GPA was very good. No problem, I thought—with the overwhelming support of my daughters and husband, I was again on the launchpad. I was accepted to the program, but a large district hired me to be the principal of a low-performing inner-city school the same week. My heart knew I couldn't do both, so I chose the school over my higher education ambitions.

It was the right thing to do. These teachers and kids needed me, and after two years of blood, sweat, and tears, they became a state-recognized school. I give all credit to the teachers. They were a fantastic group of professionals. These teachers and students became my purpose for seeking the terminal degree. The experience left me with many questions about how principals can transform failing schools. I was on fire to find the answers to my endless questions!

The school district announced they were partnering with a university to hold doctoral classes in the district office. Here was my chance. I applied and was accepted. I continued working as a principal and took classes at night. It was so hard. I began to allow the stress to affect my physical and emotional health. Something had to happen so I didn't severely damage my health or relationships. One day, a professor I had worked with at the university where I was the teacher in residence called and asked why I wasn't in their doctoral program. He had moved to that university's main campus with a new program. Five of my doctoral classmates met with him and the faculty. We transferred to this program. Ironically, this was the first university I wanted to attend, but I had chickened out.

I resigned from my principal job and accepted a job at the university as a graduate assistant for the program. I spent that year working on my dissertation and being a general helper to all the professors. When I graduated, I was offered a full-time faculty job. I have worked with doctoral students for over 11 years as their instructor, dissertation chairperson, or committee member. I have helped create a new doctorate program at one university and helped develop policies for another. I have worked with hundreds of professionals seeking this degree, which is very rewarding.

Your journey will be different. People of influence will pour into you and encourage you to do something you thought impossible. My list of mentors is numerous, and I would not be doing this fantastic job today if I had not allowed them to push me beyond my self-made limits.

—Julie Fernandez, EdD

EDS, EDD, AND PHD—WHAT IS THE DIFFERENCE?

According to the US Census Bureau:

> Since 2000, the number of people aged 25 and over whose highest degree was a master's has doubled to 21 million. The number of doctoral degree holders has more than doubled to 4.5 million. About 13.1 percent of U.S. adults have an advanced degree, up from 8.6 percent in 2000.

(2019)

INTRODUCTION TO EDUCATION DOCTORAL PROGRAMS

The National Center for Science and Engineering Statistics (NCSES) has been tracking the number of adults seeking terminal degrees in the United States since 1991. In 2021, 8.1% of all doctorate degrees were in education, and 70% of those earning an education doctorate were women. Of the 2,962 US citizens whose education doctorate was awarded in 2021, 5.3% were Asian, 9.58% were Hispanic, 17.28% were Black/African American, and 61.1% were White. In 2021, 496 non-US citizens were conferred a doctorate (NCSES, 2022).

According to the Council of Graduate Schools (2010), 50% of terminal degree seekers leave the program. The percentage of people who earn an education doctorate has dropped just over 9% since 2011. However, with the increase of online and cohort programs, universities are betting that more and more people inside and outside the field of education will seek this terminal degree.

You will hear many academics refer to doctoral degrees as "terminal degrees." *Terminal* means you cannot get a higher degree past the doctorate, and no, it does not refer to the possibility that you will die in the process.

Before getting into the weeds of a doctorate program, make sure you apply for the degree that best fits your professional goals. A standard degree offered online and on campuses is the EdS. An EdS stands for "education specialist." Universities offer this degree in different areas of study. An EdS is not a doctorate, and you will not be a "doctor" when you graduate. You will gain specialized knowledge about your area of study and be able to lead curriculum teams or be a mid-level leader, like a principal. Some school districts offer stipends or salary adjustments for people who earn this degree. This degree is not terminal and generally requires 30–65 hours of study, depending on the specialization or university. If you change your mind and decide that you want the doctorate or terminal degree, some of the hours in the EdS will be transferred, but the number of hours depends on each university's policies on transfer credits.

The EdD, or doctor of education, is a practitioner's degree that prepares educators to be practice-oriented leaders in education, which is typically—but not exclusively—reserved for pre-K–12 or higher education settings. This degree has become popular with people outside the education field. Business leaders, nurses, law enforcement, government, military, and nonprofit leaders are seeking a degree, but it is usually in the field of leadership. Many programs offer EdD in curriculum and instruction, technology, and leadership. Some programs offer avenues for certifications, such as principalship and superintendency. Others are non-certification programs. An EdD student's purpose for study is to problem-solve an issue affecting their profession. Their purpose could be to leverage change in their organization. It is a combination of research and applied practice in the field.

> **SNAPSHOT**
>
> An EdS or a doctorate? For Kelley, hindsight may have led her in a different direction.

I got my specialist degree in educational leadership from the University of Alabama. The professor I was close with encouraged me to roll some of my classes over and start on my doctorate. I took her advice. If I had it to do over again, I would not have gotten the specialist degree and went right on to the doctorate degree.

What can you do with an EdD? A student was one of the coordinators for literacy instruction in his district. The district elementary schools were evenly divided on which literacy program should be used in schools. His study was to find out which program made the most significant difference in student achievement scores for every demographic. The data was remarkable. One program showed a significant difference in student achievement. When he presented his findings to the school board, the other program was discontinued, saving the district millions of dollars.

Another student worked for the HR department of her organization. She studied a mindfulness application and tested the effectiveness of stress relief for those practicing mindful exercises. As COVID-19 began one year later, she was equipped with research and evidence to support using the mindfulness app for her coworkers. During a time of high stress and difficulty, she was able to make a difference. The timeliness of her study and dissertation work could not have been better!

The PhD focuses heavily on the pursuit of research and scholarly work. Their purpose is to seek gaps in the literature, generate new knowledge about the topic, and at times, create new theories based on their findings. Many people with PhDs seek research and teaching positions at universities.

There are times when there is a small amount of rivalry between those people who have an EdD and those who have a PhD. The question of who has the more prodigious degree is expected. We do not join in on those arguments, since when it is all said and done, we are all still referred to as "doctors." Both terminal degrees can lead to leadership and university or college teaching jobs. Some universities, though, will only hire PhDs, so check before you apply. We will go into more detail about seeking university positions in Chapter 13.

The number of credit hours for an EdD or PhD varies from 60 to 120, depending on the specialty. The courses are divided into categories. There are core, specialty area, research core, and dissertation hours. The number of years it takes to complete a terminal degree is based on two factors. Cohort programs have a tight schedule of course offerings, and students who stay within the timeline of course offerings usually spend 3–4 years. The other factor is purely in the student's head. Taking breaks from courses or not completing their research can push some students up to ten years to complete their degree.

You must stay within the ten-year line.

Most universities do not recognize courses over ten years, so you would end up retaking courses. That equates to more tuition. Every semester, you are working on your research, including tuition costs. That can add up over time to be an expensive result of a student's procrastination.

One of the newest phenomena is that most students seeking a terminal degree work full-time jobs. Back then, people quit their jobs to focus on graduate degrees. In the state of the current economy, that is only sometimes possible. I could take a year off while I completed the dissertation part of my degree, but there were many sacrifices my husband and I had to make to pay the bills. Juggling work and family life while working on this degree is very stressful. Again, I am not trying to dissuade you from seeking the degree, but you should be fully aware of the sacrifices you will have to make.

No one enters this program intending to quit, procrastinate research, or be ABD (all but dissertation).

Research by Jacks et al. (1983) cited nine reasons someone will not complete their doctoral program:

- Financial difficulties
- Poor working relationship with advisor or committee
- Substantive problems with dissertation research
- Personal or emotional problems
- Receipt of an attractive job offer
- Interference of paid work with dissertation work
- Family demands
- Lack of peer support
- Loss of interest in earning a doctorate

(p. 75)

All these problems are like brick walls that hinder many from completing their classes or dissertations and walking across the stage to receive the coveted diploma. Students who did not complete their doctorate had issues relating to the writing of the dissertation, along with feelings of isolation during the process. It is discouraging when you see your classmates finish and you are still working on your paper.

One wise person once said, "It is not about how smart you are but whether you can find the paths around the brick walls." In the spirit of such intelligent determination, let us work together to navigate this process so you can achieve success.

PLANNING WHERE YOU WANT TO GO

SNAPSHOT 📷

The doctoral journey can be overwhelming and even frustrating, as it often requires great personal demands of and sacrifices by the student, their friends, their family, their careers, etc. I can remember occasions when my family would be enjoying time during social gatherings and outings but I would need to excuse myself to work on coursework or research or writing. One such time was on a day when my wife and I, along with another family, took our young children on a fun-filled trip to Sesame Place.

My "fun" for a portion of that day was not spent enjoying the rides, games, or anything else at the theme park. To make the trip myself, I knew I would need to sacrifice somehow. I decided to carve out some time during a trip to the park to complete my doctoral work. After lunch on one of the days we were at Sesame, I remained in the quick service restaurant, pulled out my laptop, connected to the park's public Wi-Fi network, and got to work.

I can't remember at this point exactly how much time it took me, but let's assume that my sacrifice/trade-off was to spend two to three hours less time at the park and put it toward my work rather than having to miss the entire trip. I thought it was a pretty fair trade, considering I still got to make the trip and was able to simply rejoin the rest of the group later in the afternoon.

My advice for current and aspiring doctoral students and students is two-fold. For one, like I did when my family visited Sesame Place, you must learn to value and prioritize your time in such a way as to ensure that you still live your best life while hopefully completing all your work and submitting it on time. Secondly, I encourage doctoral students to enjoy and celebrate every milestone they reach and every achievement they accomplish.

There are many steps to the doctoral process, or hurdles in getting to the finish line, if you prefer to think of it that way. From first getting accepted into a doctoral program to completing the coursework, submitting or

> defending a research proposal to gain IRB approval earning student status and obtaining a committee, beginning to conduct research and analyze the data collected, to submitting dissertations drafts (and there will likely be many) and, of course, the final defense and publication of the dissertation.
>
> Enjoy these milestones and achievements for what they are worth. Each one requires lots of hard work, personal demands, and sacrifices. Of course, I cannot tell you how to celebrate these wins; I can only ask that you do. And if you do, you may find, as I did, that they are what make the journey worth it. We all know how special the result is when your work is published and you have the degree, but the journey can still be pretty great, too!
>
> —Dan Kreiness, EdD

FINANCIAL COMMITMENT

A doctorate is expensive. I have no other way to state that fact. Depending on your school of choice, it could cost you $30,000 to $60,000. Some scholarships are out there if you contact the financial aid office at the university. Veterans get significant scholarships. Some school districts give special scholarships. You must hunt. Fill out the Free Application for Federal Student Aid (FAFSA) to help apply for financial aid. Resources for graduate grants and scholarships can also be found at the College Board's Scholarship search tool, Sallie Mae's database, and Fast Web. It is common for doctoral students to quit the program due to financial barriers. Tuition is not the only cost. Ask about fees, textbooks, and editorial charges.

Are you going to hire a babysitter while you are in classes? What about gas? The first college I was accepted to required us to attend campus for classes one weekend a month. Gasoline was outrageous then, and I was 200 miles from the school. I also had to figure out the cost of a hotel on those weekends. On football game weekends, the price of hotel rooms was way above my budget. These costs, along with tuition, fees, and books, were another reason I did not attend this program.

Another hidden cost is finding an editor for your paper who is very knowledgeable about APA formatting. Editors charge by the page. You will need an editor for different stages of your research writing process, not just at the end. Papers should be error-free for all submissions. Universities do not force you to get an editor, but it is highly recommended even if you are a proficient writer. Some universities have on-site editors, but a fee may be attached to your bill if you use that service.

You will have costs for submitting your final paper for your dissertation to an online publishing company. You may buy a hardback copy of your research. The graduation regalia (cap, gown, and hood) is costly. The university's regalia may cost you hundreds of dollars. Some universities have rentals, but that may cost you over $100. Invest in the regalia if you plan to teach in higher education or are a superintendent attending many graduation ceremonies. Higher ed faculty wear their regalia multiple times a year. Yes, you can buy one that is not university-specific online, but that is up to you. There are also times when the cost is associated with the money spent and the sacrifices made.

SNAPSHOT

One contributor noted:

I work at a university and benefit from a generous education assistance program. I took one semester of doctoral work. Got straight As. Unfortunately, although the degree was "free," there was a high cost to my family. As a director, wife, and mother of four children, I was disappointed that the program didn't allow me to take one course at a time. It was a cohort model with a lock-step curriculum. I'm glad that I was admitted and had the opportunity to prove to myself that I could do it, but I'm even more grateful that I realized—after only one semester—that this was not sustainable.

Her recommendation for those considering a doctorate is:

Make sure you are in the right season of your life to start the program. Consider what sacrifices, known and unknown, you are willing to make. Be prepared to work hard (I did!), but know your non-negotiables and allow yourself to change course.

SUMMARY

The decision to take the following steps in higher education can be difficult if you do not research the type of degree you want and the professional reasons for obtaining the degree. The pressure for getting a doctorate should not be from outside forces but from within your desire to grow as a professional and researcher. The skills you learn in these programs will be used in professional settings, such as researching the best approaches to leading and learning in your professional environment.

You will become an expert in your field of study, and people will access your knowledge to make organizational decisions. It would be best to get a doctorate for many reasons, but the biggest reason is based on your career aspirations.

TRAVEL JOURNAL

- Reflect on your personal and professional aspirations and why getting a doctorate would be a good decision for you at this time in your career.
- What new knowledge or skills do you believe you will gain if you achieve a doctorate?
- Where do you see yourself professionally five years after obtaining a doctorate?
- Is getting a doctorate degree the only way you can achieve your professional goals?
- Is the decision to seek a doctorate degree coming from your need to expand your knowledge base or from outside influencers? Explore the core reasons you are seeking this degree.

PACKING CHECKLIST

- Research the type of degree (EdD or PhD) that best fits your professional goals.
- Determine whether your budget can support your degree expectations.
- Seek scholarships.

REFERENCES

Council of Graduate Schools. (2010). Ph.D. completion project: Policies and practices to promote student success. Retrieved from https://www.phdcompletion.org/quantitative-data/#

Doctorate Recipients from U.S. Universities. (2021). *National Center for Science and Engineering Statistics (NCSES) Directorate for Social, Behavioral and Economic Sciences National Science Foundation* (pp. 23–300). NSF.

Jacks, P., Chubin, D. E., Porter, A. L., & Connolly, T. (1983). The ABCs of ABDs: A study of incomplete doctorates. *Improving College and University Teaching, 31*(2), 74–81.

Chapter 2

Which Program Fits My Professional Goals?

CHAPTER OBJECTIVES

- Analyze personal professional goals.
- Connect professional goals with appropriate doctoral program.
- Determine if personal learning styles match program delivery systems, that is, on campus or through online programs.

INTRODUCTION

What are your ultimate professional goals? Focusing on your professional goals is the starting point for deciding your desired degree. If you want a doctorate to move up and influence your organization, then an EdD is fine. You can also teach college-level courses in your specialty. If your degree is in curriculum and instruction, you can work in district-level leadership positions and teach curriculum and instruction courses for undergraduate and graduate students. You can be a consultant, especially in your field of research.

If you want a doctorate to expand research in a specific field, write papers and books, and teach college-level courses, a PhD might be your choice. It does not mean an EdD cannot do research or write books, but the focus of most PhD graduates is research. Both the EdD and PhD graduates can seek district leadership roles, such as director or superintendent; gain tenure-track university positions; and influence the broader professional community by their attention to researching answers to issues in our society.

UNIVERSITY OPTIONS

With the abundance of on-campus and online doctorate programs being offered in the United States, which one fits your professional goals? Many select local or familiar schools that they attended for master's or undergraduate degrees.

WHICH PROGRAM FITS MY PROFESSIONAL GOALS?

The allegiance to your alma mater is strong. There are many choices from schools that advertise on TV or social media. It is essential to evaluate each program individually, even if it is your alma mater.

Questions to consider while choosing a university program:

- What is your professional goal?
- What interest area do you have?
- What mode of learning do you feel comfortable using—campus-based or online?
- What is your budget?
- What is your timeline for completion?

Once you narrow down your choices, check the accreditation of each campus. The university websites must share the accreditation status. Accreditation organizations are independent, third-party reviewers that monitor the curriculum, programs, faculty credentials, and student services provided by the universities or colleges in their purview. The standards are very high, and each campus under that specific accreditation organization must submit reports every few years for approval. Any new program must undergo an intensive review before it is approved. It is a checks-and-balances system that gives students assurances that the university or college is legitimate. There are great universities out there that are not accredited; however, if you are spending a lot of money and time on a degree, you want to be a graduate from one that has the professional and academic seal of approval.

The following are common university accreditation organizations:

- Accrediting Commission for Community and Junior Colleges (ACCJC)
- Western Association of Schools and Colleges
- Higher Learning Commission (HLC)
- Middle States Commission on Higher Education (MSCHE)
- New England Commission of Higher Education (NECHE)
- Northwest Commission on Colleges and Universities (NWCCU)
- Southern Association of Colleges and Schools Commission on Colleges (SACSCOC)
- WASC Senior College and University Commission (WSCUC)

Attending an accredited, highly respected university comes into play if you consider higher education your career path. Curriculum vitae (CV) are reviewed by multiple people when you apply for a teaching position at a university. If any of the reviewers find out that you are from a non-accredited university, they may not recommend you to be interviewed. The higher education community is an insular group, and universities that need to be accredited or are considered diploma factories may hurt your future chances.

> **SNAPSHOT**
>
> An applicant sought a teaching position at a university. She was very experienced in her field and had outstanding qualifications, except she received her doctorate degree from an unaccredited university. There was a lot of debate among the search committee and university leadership about whether she would qualify as a faculty member based on the policies of our accreditation organization. Every university that is accredited must submit their faculty's credentials to document that each person teaching is highly qualified, that is, has the graduate hours in the field which they would teach and an appropriate degree for the level they would be teaching. The fact that she didn't have a degree from an accredited university posed a significant problem. The university was able to hire her based on her other qualifications; however, this was an exception, and the university had to report the issue to their accreditation association every year.
>
> —anonymous university leader

Choosing the right school is the key to your success. Read reviews carefully. Not every student is happy with every program, so read the reviews critically. Students' complaints range from "the classes are boring" to "the classes are too hard." There are complaints about class times, workload, inconvenient exam times, and inflexible faculty concerning assignment due dates. This degree is not intended to be convenient or easy, so do not be naïve. Do pick the school if it has an excellent reputation for customer service or if the graduation rate is reasonable, that is, 60–90%. Graduation rates that are too high—100%—mean the curriculum may not be rigorous, and some may regard the degree as invalid. Graduation rates under 50% are unfortunate. Why would I go somewhere I have a low chance of completion? Do your homework and be cold-blooded when you choose a school.

CAMPUS-BASED

Campus-based programs mean you go to a campus to take the classes. This statement seems too obvious, but people often ask, Do I have to live near the school? Yes and no.

WHICH PROGRAM FITS MY PROFESSIONAL GOALS?

There are various ways a university sets up its class schedule, considering that most students work full-time jobs.

As you shop for a university, inquire about class meeting days and times. Do classes meet weekly? If so, how often, and what are the class times? Some schools offer weekend classes or ask students to come one weekend a month. Other campuses offer a hybrid system, so some classes meet on campus and online. There are course meetings or exams that happen outside of the regular schedule. Comprehensive exams are often on the weekends. When you begin presenting your research study, the meetings happen during the week, and you may have to take a day or half a day off to present to your committee. You must maintain your belief that classes, seminars, or presentations only happen on the specific day you meet with your classes. You also should not expect the university to work around your employment schedule.

Benefits often associated with campus-based programs can be significant. Often, meeting face-to-face with colleagues can feel more collaborative. Students may enjoy the natural feel of connecting with classmates in a classroom setting. The relationship between faculty and student can also feel more comfortable in a campus-based program. Gaining insights from a professor after seeing and hearing verbal and nonverbal communication may provide greater comfort and relational support for the student.

Campus-based programs provide additional benefits, such as fewer distractions and hands-on learning. The college campus generally provides a learning environment void of many typical distractions. Children crying, dogs barking, and ringing doorbells are minimized on college campuses. Many students credit less distraction with greater productivity, making campus-based programs more appealing. The campus-based environment may provide greater access to hands-on learning for those who consider themselves kinesthetic learners. Activities, projects, and classroom interactions that increase kinesthetic engagement will be beneficial for some. A campus-based program may be best if you prefer interaction and interpersonal communication with other students and faculty.

SNAPSHOT

A student was a full-time teacher in a district that was two hours from campus. He commuted to the evening classes and was often late to class. The faculty were gracious to him and didn't make a big deal about his late arrivals. When he got to the point where he was working on his dissertation, he expected his chair to only meet with him after 4:00 p.m. He would often call his chair late in the evenings. The chair was accommodating at first, but then the student expected his chair to respond on the weekends and very late at night. The final straw was when the student was ready to propose his research study. He demanded that the presentation take place at 7:00 p.m. on a Friday. The chair and the committee refused to accept this day and time and told him he would have to give his presentation during working hours (9:00 a.m.–5:00 p.m.). The student became belligerent and demanded the committee to conform to his schedule, not theirs. The committee refused again. Some of the committee members decided to abandon the student, thus leaving him high and dry, without a committee. He tried to get other faculty members to work with him, but his reputation for being unreasonable and disrespectful to faculty preceded him. He finally found faculty to work with him with the understanding that he would be respectful to the faculty's time and boundaries. He learned that this degree depends on working with faculty not making them work for him.

—anonymous professor

Semesters or terms have differing numbers of weeks at various institutions. Some are the 14-week standard schedule, while others are 7 or 8 weeks long. Summer is a time when many programs hold classes, so do not make vacation plans. There are usually a few weeks between semesters to go on little vacations. No faculty member will excuse you from class for a Disney week of fun. If you are committed to this journey, commit fully.

SNAPSHOT

When it came to choosing a university, I opted for one that prioritized faith-based education. The idea of incorporating religious beliefs into learning and leadership greatly appealed to me, as it allowed me to receive a well-rounded education while also nurturing my spiritual growth. The university provided me with ample resources and support to help me achieve my academic and personal goals. Thanks to faith-based education, I now have a broader perspective of the world and view it more optimistically. Additionally, by adopting a perspective based on the Bible's teachings, I have learned to prioritize others' needs before my own, accept people for who they are, and show genuine care and compassion to those around me—all in a servant leadership style.

I ultimately decided to attend college in person after much consideration. The resources available on campus, such as libraries and study areas, were a significant factor in my decision. These resources proved essential to my academic success. I was also eager to interact face-to-face with other students and make new friends. Although online courses have benefits, the lack of physical interaction challenged my ability to focus and achieve my full potential. Distractions such as cell phones, telephones, and family members surrounding me were some challenges I faced with online learning. Attending in-person classes helped eliminate these distractions and enabled me to concentrate on learning. This kept me engaged and allowed me to attain my academic goals.

—Isreal Suprano Kinlaw, EdD

ONLINE

MY STORY

I obtained my doctoral education between 2008 and 2012. During this time, online courses were gaining popularity but were still offered infrequently and often considered inadequate. In fact, because of the stigma attached to online courses, I remember the first hybrid course that I took. I questioned the way that it would be viewed on my transcript and wondered if others would think less of my degree. I wondered if the faculty would be engaging or if there would be any opportunity to communicate with colleagues. If only I had known then what I know now, I could have recognized my own errors in thought. Recognizing the strengths and challenges with each context and knowing your own strengths will assist you in this process. Here are some truths that I have learned since that first course I took:

1. Transcripts do not typically indicate the format in which a course is taken; a transcript indicates courses taken and final grades, but whether a course is hybrid, online, or in person is not often indicated. So unless the institution is a fully online institution, it is possible someone may not know if their degree was obtained online or in person.
2. A great course or amazing faculty may be found in any environment. Online or campus-based, the platform, when used effectively, may be just as engaging, and the faculty may be just as personable.
3. Graduating with a doctoral degree often has less to do with finding the right institutional fit and more to do with being the right person. Though it is important to find a program that aligns with your values and fits your practical needs (cost, location, modality, etc.), in the end, success is dependent upon YOU completing all necessary components of the program. So knowing your strengths and weaknesses, and how those will align with the program that you seek, may be even more crucial than finding the "right" institution.

—Krista Allison, PhD

For many years, online learning has been attached to some stigma. In many ways, the COVID-19 pandemic forced the acceptance of online learning, and for a time, online learning became the only option for many who wished to continue their educational journey. With only one option, stigma quickly diminishes. So during the pandemic, when nearly every institution met virtually, online learning became accepted and expected.

Online programs offer great benefits for some learners. Self-paced courses and flexibility allow many students to complete a doctoral program at a comfortable speed and convenient time. Flexibility and the ability to complete coursework at your pace may be critical if you work full-time with other responsibilities. Several single moms I have worked with would only have had the opportunity to earn a doctoral degree if the coursework had been asynchronous. They did much of their work late at night and on weekends.

Online programs may also be more accessible, inclusive, and cost-effective. If you have access to the Internet and a computer, you can access and be included in any online program. Unlike limitations of space or location associated with a traditional classroom setting, few accessibility or inclusion problems occur in the online classroom. The cost-effectiveness of online programming is also attractive to many doctoral students. In some institutions, discounts are provided for those taking online courses.

PROGRAM QUALITY AND SUPPORT

Most of my childhood was spent in Florida, so when I picture a beach, those are the beaches I picture: white sand, palm trees, picturesque environment. However, as I have traveled, I have realized that "beach" means different things to different people. My husband and I moved to Missouri during our early careers and settled in Osage Beach. Though the name is deceptive (since Missouri is not a coastal state), the "public beaches" one can visit are even more deceptive. Imagine brown rocks, murky water, and a tiny sliver of "sand" between the grass and the lake. This small piece of sand is the "beach" to many Missourians.

Beaches are not all created equally, and neither are online programs. Some online programs are like those Florida beaches, well-run with technological support, courses that promote student engagement, networking opportunities, and transparency. Other online programs are more like those Missouri beaches. But in the end, a Missouri beach is better than no beach at all!

If you are considering a doctoral degree with an online format, program quality is paramount. Some key areas to focus on include accreditation, transparency, course design, technology, and student services. Knowing the right questions to ask may assist in knowing if the online program is solid. Here are some examples of questions to consider:

1. "Who is your accrediting body?" As noted in the previous chapter, some accreditors are more stringent and expect higher standards, so do some research regarding the accreditor they mention. Accrediting bodies are the "enforcing officers" of quality in education, so choosing a suitable program starts with understanding who accredits the institution.
2. "Can I see a syllabus and course description?" Some institutions standardize course syllabi (to ensure that all EDUC 700 courses have the same material covered). In contrast, others allow faculty to create a more personalized experience. However, either way, the institution should have a process for providing an example of a course description and a syllabus (which should align). Check to see if the course description matches the syllabus. In the syllabus, note the diversity of assignments and communication. Would the format provide an engaging environment and promote connection with colleagues and faculty?
3. "What types of technology do your courses utilize?" The platform is essential (Blackboard or Canvas are the most popular), but the types of technology that faculty incorporate into courses and assignments are even more critical. An engaging atmosphere in an online environment needs various tools and technology, like Articulate 360, to assist faculty and students. Simulation software can also be beneficial for specific courses. Understanding your learning style will be beneficial (more on this in an

upcoming chapter). Knowing what tools and technology are available to faculty can help you as you consider the option of online programs and what styles of learning work best for you.
4. "Tell me about technological support for students." Regardless of whether you are a digital native, the odds are likely that if you choose to pursue a doctoral degree online, something (technology-related) will go wrong within the coming years. When it does, knowing what supportive technological resources you have is essential.
5. "What student services are offered to your online doctoral students?" Many institutions offer career services or counseling services to online doctoral students. In the coming years, these may be valuable, so knowing what is available may assist you in deciding what program is best for you.

Online doctoral programs have become very popular. The sell is that you can work at your own pace from the comfort of your home. I have created online doctoral courses and taught a few, so I am okay with this mode of instruction. What does worry me are people that need more discipline to work online.

There are weekly deadlines for assignments, and if the course is asynchronous, you do not meet with your faculty members or other classmates during the course. Asynchronous learning is designed to allow you to complete assignments on your own time, so courses of this nature demand self-disciplined students. Synchronous courses mean you have a set time to meet with your class, and you may hear a lecture or interact with the faculty and other students.

Classwork may seem more extensive in an online environment due to the nature of the limitations associated with the online environment. You will have a few activities, that is, watch a lecture, watch some videos, read textbook chapters, and read research articles, per week to complete. Then you will complete one or two assignments or take a quiz on what you did in the activities. You must be very disciplined to do the work independently and complete the assignments by the due date, which could be weekly. You cannot procrastinate. Deductions for late assignments are real. I had an online student who did not turn in any assignments all semester until one week before the course ended. He said he was a busy businessman and traveled weekly. He sent all 15 assignments to me two days before the final grades were due. I refused to grade any of it. He failed the class. His lack of urgency to complete assignments on time was no excuse and was unfair to the other students who worked diligently to meet the deadlines.

Investigate the online program to understand how the faculty and systems will support you during the research and dissertation writing process. Coursework completion may be accomplished in an online environment; often, students suggest the due dates, and course sequence is helpful in their effort to keep going. However, when you get to the dissertation phase, do you have the discipline to keep going when there are no deadlines and your support system is online? Writing a dissertation or completing a final project demands communication between the student and the faculty member.

It is critical to develop relationships early with the faculty member and determine the process so you can finish on your timeline.

COHORT SYSTEMS

Cohort systems have become very popular in campus-based and online university programs. The recruitment of doctoral students only happens once or twice a year. If accepted to a cohort, you will attend classes as a group. You get to know each other through all the courses you take together. It is an excellent opportunity to network with other local or state leaders. Universities with cohort systems of acceptance may or may not accept you if you try to join in the middle of the program or are coming in with transfer credits. You can always ask, however. While working with the same group of students in your cohort can be an excellent way to gain your reputation as a professional, it can also hurt you if you are not a team player or have a negative attitude. In one cohort, a student criticized other students' work, bad-mouthed the faculty behind their backs, and was generally unpleasant. He began looking for leadership positions in area school districts after he graduated. His reputation preceded him, and no one considered him a good student for an upper leadership position. He left the state to find people who did not know him. The influence of leaders in the field of education is a lot stronger than most people think. No matter what degree field you seek, your reputation is built by how you work with others and the quality of your work.

TRANSFER CREDITS

If you are already in a doctoral program, or if you dropped out of a program, you could continue the journey at another university. Transferring your credit hours is common and is not difficult to do. The first thing to do is contact the graduate director or the department chair of the doctoral program. They will want to review your official transcripts to match classes that are like the ones you took. Some policies limit the number of hours that can be transferred and the age of the courses. Many hours could be transferred to a new program, saving you money and time. Many universities have a ten-year rule, that is, the classes you took should have occurred within the past ten years.

Most universities only transfer doctoral courses; however, some accept courses with master's degrees. Transferring master's degree hours is unusual since the level of expectation is different. There is competition among universities to get as many students as possible, so the options for transferring schools are available. Some universities will not accept course transfers if the grades are pass/fail rather than actual grades. It is hard to determine a GPA from pass/fail scoring.

Exploring your options and getting as many credit hours as possible does not hurt. If you do not ask, you will not know if it is possible. Each university has its policies, so double-check their transfer hours policies and procedures.

SUMMARY

Selecting a university is one of the most important decisions you will make. Analyzing whether you go to a campus-based program or an online program is a personal decision that involves how you learn and manage time. If you are a person who needs the routine of scheduled classes and personal interaction with other students and faculty, you may need to pick a campus-based program. However, online programs may be better if you are organized and comfortable with technology and your work schedule is mired in last-minute demands at all hours. Some universities offer both on-campus and online programs, and it may be possible to move from one to the other. Check the university policies before making a significant change. The choice of programs is up to you; do not feel pressured to pick a program that does not fit your lifestyle or learning style.

TRAVEL JOURNAL

Eliminate your thoughts on the convenience of the programs and reflect on what type of learner you are now.

- Are you someone that needs personal interaction, or are you comfortable with online communication as a way of building professional and academic relationships?
- What are your strengths and weaknesses in time management?
- What is your timeline for completing this degree?
- How many courses are you comfortable taking each semester, considering your professional and personal obligations?
- What personal habits will you have to develop to meet the course requirements in this degree?

PACKING CHECKLIST

- Compare university programs to determine which one best fits your professional goals, timeline, and budget.

University	Program Title	PhD or EdD	Online or on-campus	Meeting days and times	Credit Hours	Cost	Years to complete

- Find out the transfer credit policies for the university of choice.
- What accreditation organization is associated with the university of choice?

Part II
Packing Your Skills Suitcase

Chapter 3

Assessing Your Skills

CHAPTER OBJECTIVES

- Reflect upon how personal experience affects adult learning.
- Evaluate your learning style as an adult learner and plan your studying and reading assignments based on your learning style.
- Analyze personal organizational skills.
- Evaluate academic writing skills.
- Evaluate academic reading skills.

INTRODUCTION

Now is the time to examine the bag of knowledge and skills you will need for this journey. Most doctoral students are over 30, far removed from the time-rich years of their undergraduate degree. Juggling a full-time job, family, friends, and outside interests can be overwhelming when adding to the demands of a high-level graduate program. If you have not been reading research, writing academic-level papers, or studying for tests in the past few years, you will have to dust off the study and organizational skills that you shelved many years ago. The chances that you can still study and write late at night or pull all-nighters are unrealistic. We are not our younger selves, and our brains may be overloaded with endless information that has nothing to do with our research. Setting priorities and boundaries is imperative for survival. Revitalizing basic skills of organization, study, writing, reading, and statistics at this stage of your life is the key to success. What worked for you when you were young may not work for you now. The high expectations of the assignments will not give you the advantage to procrastinate or turn in weak material because you are "just too busy." We must evaluate how we learn as adults compared to how we learn as teenagers or young adults.

ADULT LEARNING THEORY

When you begin your search for the ultimate topic for your research, the foundation of the research must be embedded with a theory.

Abend (2008) defines one type of research-based theory as "an original 'interpretation,' 'reading,' or 'way of making sense' of a certain slice of the empirical world" (p. 178). While many in the field of education are familiar with the theory of *pedagogy* as the way we teach children, the theory of *andragogy* is based on how we teach adults. As you consider a doctoral degree and begin considering topics, understanding the principles of andragogy is paramount. The amount of experience you have had as an adult learning significantly affects how today you learn vs. how you learned material as a teenager or even as a young adult.

> **SNAPSHOT**
>
> Back in high school, I wasn't challenged often and therefore relied more on memory retention for lessons, but as I've grown older and realized that so much of that knowledge was never truly retained beyond the final exams, I've changed my style to repetition and then application of the lessons. I take a lot of notes because I am also a creative person. I love to personalize them with drawings, fun colors, and even stickers to make reviewing the information later fun and not as tedious.
>
> — Mary Fernandez

Malcolm Knowles is the predominant theorist behind adult learning theory. His theory describes six principles of andragogy as being: (1) the learner needs to know; (2) the self-concept of the learner; (3) prior experience of the learner; (4) readiness to learn; (5) orientation to learning; and (6) motivation to learn (Knowles, 2005, p. 3).

Learners Need to Know Why, What, and How

Whereas children depend on adults to teach them what they need to know, adult learners are more independent and seek knowledge to understand the world at a higher level. When my daughters were young, the "why" question was forever spoken. My answers for them at that time were surface-level, an easy answer to explain why things happen as they do. "Why can't I stay up all night?" "Because you will be too tired to go to the beach tomorrow." Asked and answered.

However, adults seek a more profound understanding when they ask, "Why?" This learning process is the basis of educational research—why, what, and how

ASSESSING YOUR SKILLS

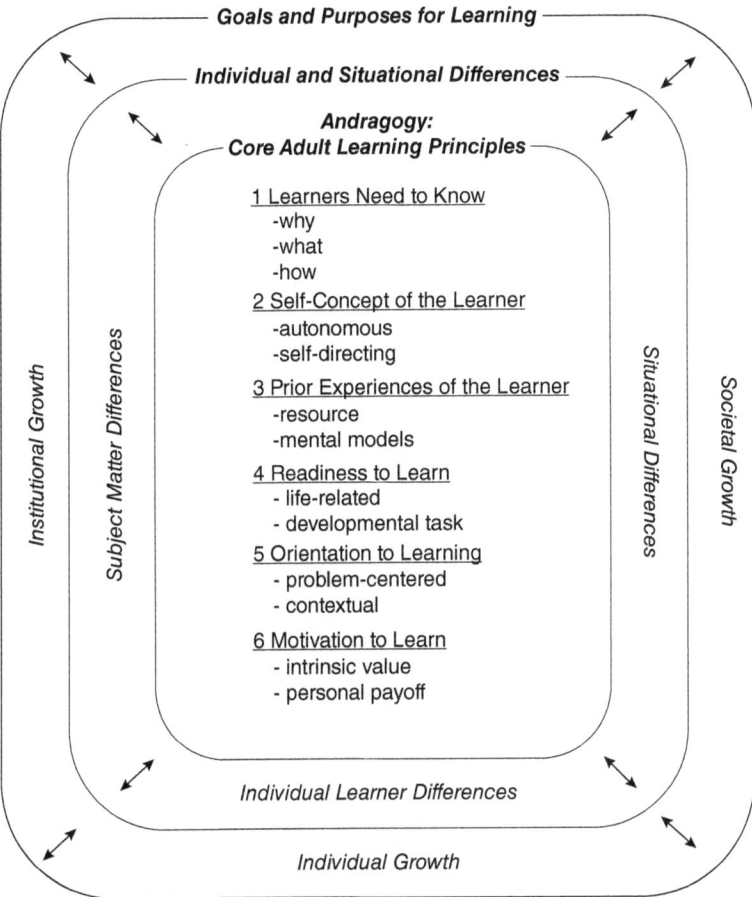

Figure 3.1 Andragogy in practice.

are the questions we seek. Why don't all students learn mathematics the same way? Why do some populations of students do better in single-gender schools than those who are not in single-gender schools? Adults are forever asking questions to deepen their understanding to find solutions. Adult learners seek the epiphany, the "Oh, that is why . . ." moment—connecting the why response to what that means in my profession to how we can lead change to fix the situation. Research is not just about writing a paper for a degree or publication but finding solutions to the big "why." You will become more motivated in your classes and research if you embrace the why and apply the answers to your professional situation.

Self-Concept of the Learner

Adult learners must be independent learners who problem-solve when facing the unknown. Children expect teachers to give them the resources they need to find answers. However, in the higher-level college experience, you must find your answers. The programs are designed to create independent thinkers, not robots. Please do not expect your professor to provide the sources of literature and research for your research or your assignments. It would be best if you did the work of searching for answers. I have had students contact me for bibliographies for their topic, especially topics I regularly write about or teach. I only sometimes share sources, because it does not help the students learn how to seek, think, and understand. If they have a glaring hole, I will question them about their sources or lack of credible sources. For example, one student wrote a paper on school culture and climate. She wrote a five-page paper but left out a prominent researcher who has written many papers and books on the topic. When I asked her about that author, she looked at me with a blank stare. I was amazed that she did not see him cited in any of the articles she used for her paper. My job as a professor, dissertation chair, and mentor is to guide rather than to give all the answers. It is like teaching a kid how to ride a bike. You can tell them the process and even hold on to the bike seat as they wobble down the sidewalk, but there is a time when you must let go. The doctorate program faculty will not hold on to your bike seat as your professors did during your undergraduate or even your master's degree. The professors may hand you a Band-Aid if you fall or cheer for you as you begin to pedal on your own, but it is critical to remember that this is your journey and your degree.

Prior Experience of the Learner

Prior experience can help or hurt a doctoral student. Too often, people rely on their personal and professional experience instead of pursuing credible research. They have preconceived perceptions about every topic based on their personal bias. On the other hand, class discussions are very dynamic when you have a group of professionals all talking about a topic from different perspectives.

What one person sees in a situation is different for everyone in the room. There can be heated discussions, especially about diversity and social justice issues.

If you have not experienced racism, how can you understand what it is like to be persecuted? If you have yet to teach in a low-poverty, high-minority school, how can you judge the teachers and leaders in that school?

The program aims to build upon what you know or have experienced and add different perspectives from different sources to your mental model.

Mental models are how you see the world and understand relationships between ideas and concepts. Mental models are ingrained and depend upon your experiences. The more you learn outside your assumptions about a topic, the more you grow as an expert. When writing about any topic you consider your area of expertise, do more research by researchers with the opposite point of view. You may disagree with them but also learn something, broadening your knowledge scope. If you only read articles that match your worldview, you will not grow; this degree is a waste of time.

Readiness to Learn

Developing mental models connects directly to readiness to learn. Are you ready to challenge your worldview with new information?

Prepare yourself to learn new concepts and theories. The doctoral students who will walk away with the most profound learning are open to expanding their perceptions and perspectives. Unfortunately, we have seen students who came in to get a degree for a pay raise or for a position they covet. They do the least amount of work they can do without failing. They write mediocre research papers and rarely participate in class discussions. They have a rigid point of view and resist growing a new mental model or worldview.

They are there for potential extrinsic rewards, not intellectual growth.

The other type of student is the one who is so excited that they cannot get enough. They are in the library, studying, and are excessively talkative in class about new concepts they have learned. They find new information and share it with anyone who will listen. This student has overcome the fear of learning new things and hopes to use the knowledge they gather during this process to make significant changes in their professional world. Do they sometimes fall on their faces when their work is not satisfactory? Yes, but they use these stumbles to make themselves stronger. They see opportunity in the failures to learn about themselves and their research topics. Readiness to learn is also overcoming the fear of failure. Everyone carries a small amount of rust on their academic brains when they enter the program. You must relearn how to write, read, and think.

SNAPSHOT

When I wrote my first paper for my first doctoral class, I had a writer's block the size of a thousand-pound boulder. I sat at my laptop and stared at it for an hour. My college-aged daughter, Sarah, came into the room and asked me what was wrong. I cried as I revealed that I felt like I wasn't smart enough for this level of work. I felt so helpless and basically stupid. She put her arms around me and said, "Just write. You can fix it later. Write what you think, research it, and fill in the citations later. No

> pressure, Mom, but Mary and I are watching you do this, and it gives us direction and hope for our future. You can do this!" Nothing like having the boulder placed on your shoulder. I did write that paper, and I did get a good grade. It was the beginning of a life of self-discovery, and yes, both my daughters are amazing women that will change the world.
>
> —Anonymous

Orientation to Learning

Orientation to learning is directly connected to why you selected the doctoral program course of study. Suppose you are in a curriculum and instruction-oriented program. In that case, your study aims to discover different ways children learn and how teachers and administrators can better meet their needs through curriculum development and instructional practices. Similarly, if you seek a degree connected to leadership, you want to become more informed of best practices for leadership in organizations and schools. Choose your course of study based on your interests. In Bloom's taxonomy language, this means higher-order thinking, such as application-, analysis-, synthesis-, and evaluation-level constructs. You are more interested in applying knowledge than just learning facts. The learning process revolves around analyzing ideas and using that knowledge to evaluate what is helpful in your professional field. Do not be surprised if you discover aspects of your topic of interest that blow your mind! I thought a good leader was a servant leader, and in that, I would spend my time serving my faculty and staff to the point of exhaustion. My research found a different perspective.

Building the leadership capacity of my faculty and staff led to higher outcomes in their performance than my doing everything for them. I still consider my leadership style as having some aspects of servant leadership; however, I realized that every leader has multiple styles that fit different situations and populations of people. The more you connect your learning to your profession, the more motivated you will be to search for new and exciting information.

Motivation to Learn

Finally, are you motivated to learn? If you plan to spend tens of thousands of your money on this degree, I sure hope so! Adults need a connection between their learning and what they want to do with the outcome—a doctorate. In this instance, motivation to improve the knowledge of your field to grow as a professional (intrinsic) is more important than a pay raise (extrinsic). You will not be guaranteed to make more money after completing this degree. There is no guarantee that you will get a promotion. How will you feel when you complete this journey? It may be the satisfaction of doing something no one in your family has ever achieved.

There will be days when you feel like this program is too hard on your body, mind, and checkbook. Maslow (1950) refers to self-actualization as a motivation for people facing a challenge of epic size. People need to feel that what they are doing will positively affect the world where they live and work. When you graduate, you can reflect on the one truth in your life—you have achieved your highest academic potential. You cannot get any higher. When I felt overwhelmed, I would consider how this research would guide me in becoming a more effective leader.

LEARNING STYLES

Educators are familiar with the typical learning styles that are used in pedagogy. Educational theorist Fleming created VARK, which has added to the list of visual, audio, and kinesthetic learning styles to include reading/writing preferences (Fleming et al., 2006). The theories surrounding learning styles have become controversial due to the limitations given in each area. People should not be boxed into one style and expected only to learn that way. Adult learners do not fit in the typical learning style paradigm as children do.

David Kolb's (1984) theory of learning cycle and styles is unique to adults' learning styles. The general principle is that learners participate in experiencing, reflecting, thinking, and acting. "Learning is the process whereby knowledge is created through the transformation of experience" (Kolb, 1984, p. 38). His theory consists of a four-stage cycle of actions or abilities: concrete experience, reflective observation, abstract conceptualization, and active experimentation. The second part of his theory connects this cycle to four learning styles: diverging, converging, assimilating, and accommodating.

The challenge with this theory is that it applies only to experiential learning and is not appropriate for memorization and information assimilation. Honey et al. (2006) expanded Kolb's theory of learning styles that includes a primary style for learning categorized as activist, reflector, pragmatist, and theorist. Both learning style theories are closely related but can give insight into your learning style as an adult learner. An *activist* is a learner with the philosophy of "I will try anything once" and tends to learn by doing. They have an open-minded approach to learning and enter new experiences without bias. A *reflector*'s philosophy is to be cautious. They tend to like to stand back and ponder experiences, collect firsthand data from others, and think about it thoroughly before concluding. A *theorist*'s philosophy is, "If it is logical, it is good," and they like to understand the theory behind actions, prefer to analyze and draw new information into a logical theory, and are keen on basic assumptions, principles, theories, models, and systems thinking. The *pragmatist*'s philosophy is, "There is always a better way" and "Good enough is enough," and they need to be able to see how to put the learning into practice in the real world and tend to be impatient with ruminating and open-ended discussions (Pratchett et al., 2016). This discussion aims to explore your learning style, whether it is Kolb's or Honey and Mumford's theories. Remember that one learning style may dominate your learning of new things, but we tend to have a combination of styles that fit different situations. Of course, learning theories are abundant, so be a theorist and explore! You can go online and take surveys to narrow down how you learn.

> **SNAPSHOT** 📷
>
> I am more curious and interested in learning. In high school and even in undergraduate, it was, at times, just jumping through hoops to earn a particular grade. Since then, I have found myself more curious and learning because I am interested in growth and future applications of the learning.
>
> —Kristie Rogers Cerling, EdD

Amponsah (2020) created a study to evaluate learning styles of adult learners in higher education and asked the following questions:

1. How do you react when you hear or come across new ideas?
2. When do you normally put new ideas into practice? How do you do that?
3. What is your approach to new situations or challenges?
4. What role(s) do you prefer to play in group discussions?
5. How do you react to people who are not organized in their activities or work?

(p. 540)

These are great, reflective questions you can ponder over coffee as you plan your journey in the doctoral program. It is best to know who you are and how you learn now vs. when you were a kid. Remember the hard truth when entering an education doctorate program: no matter your learning style, the expectation is to explore what you want to know within the context of your courses. You direct the depth of your learning experience. This process is not professor-focused, that is, the burden of gaining knowledge and skills is your responsibility, not the faculty. Finding the intrinsic value of learning at this level will motivate you to keep your focus on the endgame. Analyze your learning style as an adult and accept the changes you have experienced since your undergraduate or even during your graduate degrees. This degree is based on your understanding of yourself as a learner and researcher. The faculty assume you are a grown-up and can take care of yourself. You will not be treated as someone who needs constant support. This assumption applies to reading the syllabus for each course, reviewing rubrics before turning in assignments, and not taking shortcuts in your learning process.

SELF-EFFICACY

Can you complete this degree? Are you capable of the work? These are the fundamental questions one asks before starting something new. Albert Bandura (1995) describes *self-efficacy* as the belief in a person's "capabilities to organize and execute the courses of action required to manage prospective situations" (p. 2). This theory encompasses the motivation, emotions, and actions of someone attempting something new. Education researchers often add Bandura's theory to teacher and leadership effectiveness topics. Do teachers and leaders feel and act like they know what they are doing in their jobs? How confident do they feel, and do these feelings motivate their actions?

The theory of self-efficacy can be applied to understanding the motivations and emotions of doctoral students as they begin and progress through their program. There are moments when everyone feels less than capable when facing new learning environments. There is an expectation, both real and perceived, that all doctoral students are highly educated overachievers who are unstoppable. It would be great if that were true. Many students experience that self-doubt: "Am I able to do this?" or "What if someone finds out I am not that smart?" *Imposter syndrome* is a common affliction among doctoral students. Believing that you do not belong in a scholarly community leads to depression, procrastination in completing assignments, and dropping out of the program.

Sverdlik et al. (2020) determined that doctoral students perceived membership in a scholarly community as a negative predictor of imposter syndrome, which could manifest itself as depression, illness symptoms, and stress (p. 751). Doctoral students have a higher chance of feeling unworthy of being included in advanced programs and are less likely to accept praise. The research also indicates that if doctoral students are included in the scholarly community by presenting at conferences or co-publishing articles with their mentors, they are more likely to feel worthy of their status (Weidman et al., 2001).

Researchers at Georgia Southern University did a longitudinal study of three cohorts of education leadership doctoral students to measure their levels of self-efficacy during different stages of their program. McBrayer et al. (2021) sought to understand the efficacy of their students in terms of their ability as scholarly practitioner-researchers. They identified four trends that described the level of self-efficacy of students reported on the surveys: social support, academic challenges, discipline, effort, motivation, and personal challenges. The researchers concluded that as self-efficacy increased, so did the quality of students' research skills.

> Overall, students reported the highest levels of self-efficacy in their ability to solve problems if they invest the necessary effort, ability to remain calm when facing difficulties due to their coping abilities, and ability to manage and solve difficult problems if they try hard enough.
>
> (p. 505)

The work-family-and-academic balance was crucial for managing the feelings of self-efficacy while in the program. Waiting for faculty to respond to emails/phone calls, IRB approval, and faculty changes in their committee added stress or feelings of lack of control. Building relationships with fellow students, mentors, faculty, and committee members was crucial for helping students feel more in control and motivated to continue working through the program.

In online courses, self-efficacy plays a vital role in success. Predictors of online academic success include self-efficacy and self-regulatory behaviors (Bradley et al., 2017). Unsurprisingly, students with proficient computer skills and who interact with technology regularly are better adapted to online coursework (McCoy & McNaughton, 2021). Students may benefit from professors providing consistent, timely, and individualized feedback concerning student performance.

A student's resilient sense of efficacy can be improved through constructive feedback and guidance (Bandura, 1997; Bradley et al., 2017). In an online environment, constructive feedback, and improved self-efficacy may assist students in pursuing a doctoral degree.

SNAPSHOT

I am a more experiential learner now than I ever was back in high school and undergrad. There are obvious reasons, as I have experienced so much over the years, but it is more about a different attitude to learning. Now I want to learn to improve myself, my relationships, my work, my community, and the world. I challenge myself more now to take what I learn and apply it! It is not just learning for wisdom, but improvement.

—Salley Burbage Branch

ORGANIZATIONAL SKILLS

Organizational skills are related to how well you plan, prioritize, delegate, and manage your time. Some students make impressive color-coded "to-do" lists but are quick to get distracted from the list by someone else's emergency. You must force yourself to turn off distractions to focus on writing and research. Time management while working full-time is easier said than done, but you cannot be there for everyone if you do not prioritize yourself. As discussed in a previous chapter, family meetings must take place to explain the journey ahead of you. Everyone must pitch in to help with household duties, and you must let go and allow them to care for themselves. The way they clean the kitchen may not be to your standards, but they are teachable.

You need to consistently apply organizational skills to learn and retain the information you are learning in your classes, and you will need to complete the research project. If you are a list maker, avoid making lists on random pieces of paper that can be lost. Keep a notebook and write down due dates to prioritize the most urgent assignments. Aim to read at least one to two weekly articles on your topic. Schedule this reading or writing time on your calendar, and do not allow anyone or anything to distract you from this commitment.

Write your assignments on your calendar with a few days of leeway so you will not rush to turn them in at the last minute. Please do not rely on your memory when it comes to deadlines. You receive a syllabus at the beginning of every course, and there is little wiggle room on due dates. The university has deadlines for grades at midterm and end of the semester. Little grace is given if you turn in work late, since that adds pressure for the faculty to grade and post grades within the university deadlines. A faculty member will likely not accept late work unless you have a perfect excuse, such as a hospital stay, sick family, or a death in the family. Remember that the faculty in the program are a very close community and talk to each other about students. We had one student who had his mother die four times. No, he did not have stepmoms; he could not organize himself to turn in his assignments and thought the faculty was not keeping track.

When saving an assignment or notes on your computer, put the date on the file name so you do not turn in old paper versions. Develop files with the course name instead of the number. You will use the concepts in the file to help you study for comprehensive exams or to use in your literature review. You can organize your research articles and courses in binders or folders saved in the Cloud. Color-coding is such a lifesaver. I was old-fashioned and color-coded sub-topics when I read a research article. When I began to write about one of the sub-topics in my literature review, I searched the articles for corresponding colors, such as yellow-highlighted sentences related to transformational leadership. In contrast, green highlights were related to servant leadership.

ACADEMIC/SCHOLARLY WRITING

We live in a world of emails and text messages. Funny emojis instead of words are used even in professional situations. Many of us write as we talk. Our voice, tone, and personality are visually displayed for all to see. Unfortunately, casual writing does not have a place in academia. Academic or scholarly writing is the formal voice used during your program. For many doctoral students, this is a challenging but necessary transition. Academic or scholarly writing requires a writer to be concise, coherent, and objective.

The *Publication Manual of the American Psychological Association*, or *APA Manual* for scholarly writing is the resource most education research writers will depend upon during and after their degree. It is updated quite often, so it is best to use the most current edition of the *APA Manual*. According to the *APA Manual* 7th edition (2020), the style creates a uniform presentation of ideas in a "clear, concise and organized manner" (p. 8). All sources must be credited, and the papers must be written predictably so all researchers can report significant details of their research protocol so readers can critically read and evaluate the findings and replicate the study. The manual is a crucial resource for all your writing in your degree. Faculty expect that citations and references are written according to the manual's specifications. There is no excuse for sloppy research or the comment, "Oh, I was going to cite that later" or "I was going to rephrase that direct quote when I did my revisions." People get so caught up in their writing that sometimes they forget to cite or rephrase, which lands them in deep trouble. You are held accountable to the expectations of scholarly writing in every assignment, from online discussions to informal journal entries, especially if you quote or refer to a source. If you plan on publishing your research in a professional journal, APA style is usually expected. Peer-reviewed journals are sticklers for adherence to the formality of scholarly writing.

> **SNAPSHOT**
>
> Jesse Redlo shared a memorable moment from his doctoral program. He remembers "getting [his] first paper back with a failing grade and learning through [his] professor how to write at a scholarly level." The advice that he has is to "[s]tay humble, soak up knowledge, and recognize that a doctoral degree is the start of learning, not the end."

The formal tone of scholarly writing does not include contractions or jargon. Using terms that are colloquial or current lingo is not acceptable. You are writing a paper to explain a phenomenon to people who may need to learn the education jargon we use, and they need to comprehend the systems we have in pre-K–12 or higher education institutions.

Transitions between paragraphs and subtopics are fundamental. Refrain from fooling people by using too many lofty words you picked from a thesaurus. Any professor can tell that you are adding overly wordy or redundant sentences to meet your required word count for a paper. Be concise and get to the point of the information you are trying to impart.

> **SNAPSHOT**
>
> A student of mine turned in a research paper. It was written in such a casual voice, with sentences such as, "Hey, did you ever get a parent mad at you? It was a bummer, right?" I had to explain to him how inappropriate his writing was for an academic-level paper. I'm not sitting in a bar, having a conversation with you; I am a professor reading your paper to see if you understand the concepts you are writing about. The way you write a research paper or even an online discussion thread reflects not only your professionalism but also your capability to communicate in the professional arena.
> —anonymous professor

One of the biggest frustrations graduate faculty have with their students is their writing ability. Few students refrain from writing in general, and the quality could be better when they must write an academic paper. Poor-quality academic writing is the downfall of many doctoral students. If their writing skills are mediocre and they seek support from a writing center or editor, their chances of completing this degree are more optimistic. There is no debate here; you must write with a formal voice to succeed.

Underdeveloped writing skills are not a hill you should die upon. There is hope. Almost all universities have writing centers with skilled tutors to help support both undergraduate and graduate students. Editors can be expensive but are life-changing for many students. There are software packages and resources such as Grammarly and Purdue Owl for APA rules that can help. However, these tools will only help you if you work to improve independently.

Once you finish this degree, your reputation and the university's reputation are measured by how well you communicate verbally and in writing.

You do not want your supervisors or direct reports to roll their eyes when you write an email or a report with blaring grammar and spelling errors. The skill of formal writing is essential for all leaders in any area of education.

> **SNAPSHOT** 📷
>
> A doctoral student was in the final stages of his dissertation, but his writing skills were far from competent. His grammar and spelling were dismal. His chair and committee gave him numerous opportunities to make corrections, but few revisions took place. His goal was to give a final defense and graduate at the next ceremony. Unfortunately, because he refused to clean up his paper, he missed the deadline for graduation. He was very angry and blamed the committee for not helping him. He wrote an email to the president of the university to appeal the decision not to allow him to defend and graduate. The email to the president had so many grammar and spelling errors his appeal was quickly dismissed. The president thanked the committee for being good stewards of the high standards of the university and not allowing poor work to be accepted.
>
> —anonymous professor

READING SKILLS

You do two things more than anything else in a doctoral program: read and write. You read books and research articles and then write about them. Academic reading is also a unique voice. Everything you read, especially peer-reviewed materials, is written with a scholarly tone. The concentration you need when reading expository text such as this is much more intense than reading narrative texts. You are reading for information, and details are described that you must internalize. Reading research material demands that not only do you read for information but also read the information critically. You must decipher whether a research study is valid and reliable in its methodology. Do the results of the study match the questions the study is seeking? Is the population in the research article appropriate for drawing the correct conclusions?

Critical reading skills and selecting appropriate research to support your papers are essential for success. Instead of skimming the text, you should evaluate the consistency of the content, the connection to considerable research, and the soundness of the statistical design. For most articles, you can focus on the abstract, introduction, literature review, results, and discussion of the implications of the results. Suppose the article is connected to your future or current research. Using literature review topics and gleaning the references to expand your knowledge base is okay. I am not saying that you can copy what they wrote. That is plagiarism. Using literature reviews of research papers can give you another perspective on your topic. If you want to use a source they cited, go to the source, not just take the paraphrased interpretation of the information in that article. A big problem with students citing research is that they need to be more specific in giving credit to the researchers. They say, "Research shows . . ." What research? By whom? Be specific!

Research results cannot be rumors or vague interpretations. Go to the primary source of the research an article is citing while you are reading the article. Do not use secondary sources, that is, articles quoting or paraphrasing research. Reading research is much like archaeology; you must dig deep to find accurate answers. Do not be surface-level readers.

STATISTICS

Besides writing and reading, the biggest fear is the statistical processes you must learn and apply in your classes and research study. You will probably take quantitative, qualitative, action, and mixed research methods courses. These are the courses where students tend to struggle if they do not have a strong statistical background. The research on statistics anxiety (SA) is incredible. Yes, this is a real thing. Trassi et al. (2022) conducted a meta-analysis "on SA in university students in the context of statistical performance, individual differences in statistical learning" (p. 76). They identified that students in the humanities or social sciences are more likely to show signs of SA, resulting in a negative emotional state and cognitive disruptions in understanding the concepts. The anxiety surrounding SA affects working memory. Working memory allows people to manage multiple pieces of information during problem-solving.

Excessive worry, stress, and fear of failure can be connected to past experiences when the person was unsuccessful in an educational setting. SA can manifest itself when people perceive statistics regarding their self-efficacy and self-concept. Socio-economic experiences in education and culture can be factors for an increase in instances of people experiencing SA (Trassi et al., 2022). If you may experience SA when facing your statistical courses or choosing a methodology for your study, get help. Help is available and should support your need to conduct a viable study. Too many students choose qualitative over quantitative methodology solely because of the fear of statistics. You should choose the methodology that can best test your hypothesis and not be hindered by the anxiety of revealing your Achilles' heel. We all have weaknesses, and unfortunately, this degree has a way of exposing the best and worst of our abilities. You are not alone, so do not let any phobia stand in your way.

ACCOMMODATIONS

As educators, we should be familiar with Section 504 of the Rehabilitation Act of 1973. This act protects people with disabilities from discrimination. Higher education institutions are required by law to provide accommodations to anyone (undergraduate, graduate, or doctoral students). Section 504 requires colleges and universities to provide "reasonable accommodations" to individuals who have a disability. The law defines a person with a disability as a person

> [w]ith a physical or mental impairment that substantially limits one or more major life activities. Who has a record of such an impairment; or Who is regarded as having such impairment.
> (United States Department of Health, Education, and Welfare, Office for Civil Rights, 1978)

We have students who have dyslexia, ADHD, hearing impairments, and anxiety disorders who enter our programs and do have the right to apply for accommodations. If you would qualify for accommodations, seek out the office of student services at your university to get more information on how to qualify.

Accommodations for post–secondary education institutions are less-extensive than in Pre-K–12 settings. Extended time, testing in a quiet area, but not tutoring. To qualify for accommodations, you must provide specific types of documentation as proof of disability status. The university can provide accommodation if it is not an unfair advantage over nondisabled students.

Students whose primary language is not English also face some challenges. If you are enrolled in a university in the United States, English is the primary language, and all assignments must be written in English. Grammar and spelling rules are challenging, and it is recommended that multilingual students seek support from tutors and editors. Again, the university is not required to provide tutoring services. However, most campuses have graduate-level tutoring and editing services, so please check the university website for student services. The faculty can be accommodating; however, the final research paper must adhere to the same standards for all students, despite disability status or language differences.

SUMMARY

Before any personal growth journey, candidly assessing the skills you need to meet the goal is your first step to success. This authentic appraisal of your abilities is not intended to discourage you from starting this degree but to plan remediations for areas of weakness. You do have strengths to build upon, but sometimes we allow those skills to atrophy, become weak, or not reach the level of expectation for this level of education. Preparation before starting a doctoral program by taking writing or introductory math courses to build that brain muscle you have not used in a while can relieve the stress and give you the confidence to forge ahead. Some students work on their skills during the program, which results in a mixture of hits or misses regarding quality work. Others plan and prepare themselves before starting the program to give them the advantage of having some skills already primed for the work ahead. Only you can determine the course of your future in advanced education programs. Evaluate your learning style as an adult and adjust before you begin so you do not waste a day or assignment trying to find your footing.

TRAVEL JOURNAL

- How do you learn new skills and knowledge in comparison to how you learned as a teenager or undergraduate student?
- What do you believe is your role as a doctoral student in learning new material and skills?
- How are you planning to overcome areas of weakness in your academic skills?

PACKING CHECKLIST

- Go to online surveys to get insight on your learning styles.
- Enroll in academic writing courses if you need to improve your academic writing skills.
- Speak to the university student services coordinator in charge of accommodations if you have a disability that might require accommodations.

REFERENCES

Abend, G. (2008). The meaning of theory. *Sociological Theory*, 26, 173–199.

American Psychological Association. (2020). *Publication manual of the American Psychological Association 2020: The official guide to APA style* (7th ed.). American Psychological Association.

Amponsah, S. (2020). Exploring the dominant learning styles of adult learners in higher education. *International Review of Education*, 66(4), 531–550. https://doi.org/10.1007/s11159-020-09845-y

Bandura, A. (1995). *Self-efficacy in changing societies*. Cambridge University Press.

Bandura, A. (1997). *Self-efficacy : The exercise of control*. W.H. Freeman and Company.

Bradley, R. L., Browne, B. L., & Kelley, H. M. (2017). Examining the influence of self-efficacy and self-regulation in online learning. *College Student Journal, 51*(4), 518+. Retrieved June 25, 2023, from Gale Academic OneFile, link.gale.com/apps/doc/A519935687/AONE?u=chazsu_main&sid=bookmark-AONE&xid=bb549147.

Fleming, N., & Baume, D. (2006). Learning styles again: VARKing up the right tree! *Educational Developments, SEDA Ltd, 7*(4), 4–7.

Honey, P., & Mumford, A. (2006). *The learning styles helper's guide* (rev ed.). Peter Honey Publications.

Knowles, M. S., Holton, E. F., & Swanson, R. A. (2005). *The adult learner: The definitive classic in adult education and human resource development*. Taylor & Francis Group. ProQuest eBook Central, https://ebookcentral.proquest.com/lib/csuniv/detail.action?docID=232125.

Kolb, D. A. (1984). *Experiential learning: Experience as the source of learning and development* (Vol. 1). Prentice-Hall.

Maslow, A. H. (1950). Self-actualizing people: A study of psychological health. *Personality, Symposium, 1*, 11–34.

McBrayer, S., Fallon, K., Tolman, S., Wallace Calhoun, D., Ballesteros, E., & Mathewson, T. (2021). Examining educational leadership doctoral students' self-efficacy as related to their role as a scholarly practitioner researcher. *International Journal of Doctoral Studies, 16*, 487–512. https://doi.org/10.28945/4811

McCoy, A. & McNaughton, D. (2021). Effects of online training on educators' knowledge and use of system of least prompts to support augmentative and alternative communication. *Journal of Behavioral Education, 30*(3), 319–349. https://doi.org/10.1007/s10864-020-09374-6

Pratchett, T., & Young, G. (2016). *Practical tips for developing your staff*. Facet Publishing (Created from csuniv on 2023–05–26).

Sverdlik, A., Hall, N. C., & McAlpine, L. (2020). Ph.D. Imposter syndrome: Exploring antecedents, consequences, and implications for doctoral well-being. *International Journal of Doctoral Studies, 15*, 737–758. https://doi.org/10.28945/4670

Trassi, A. P., Leonard, S. J., Rodrigues, L. D., Rodas, J. A., & Santos, F. H. (2022). Mediating factors of statistics anxiety in university students: A systematic review and meta-analysis. *Annals of the New York Academy of Sciences, 1512*(1), 76–97. https://doi.org/10.1111/nyas.14746

United States Department of Health, Education, and Welfare, Office for Civil Rights. (1978). *Section 504 of the rehabilitation act of 1973: Fact sheet: Handicapped persons rights under Federal law*. Department of Health, Education, and Welfare, Office of the Secretary, Office for Civil Rights.

Weidman, J. C., Twale, D. J., & Stein, E. L. (2001). Socialization of graduate and professional students in higher education: A perilous passage? *ASHE-ERIC Higher Education Report, 28*(3). https://files.eric.ed.gov/fulltext/ED457710.pdf

Chapter 4

Preparing Yourself for the Road Ahead

CHAPTER OBJECTIVES

- Plan how to organize time and workspace for assignments and research.
- Understand the commitment to attending classes and completing assignments.

INTRODUCTION

In the book *Wild: From Lost to Found on the Pacific Crest Trail* by Cheryl Strayed, she describes her adventures during a three-month hike alone on the Pacific Crest Trail (PCT). Recovering from personal loss and destructive behaviors, she seeks to find meaning while hiking from New Mexico to Oregon. While she packs enough gear, she does not physically or emotionally prepare for the journey. She is blessed multiple times by people she meets along the way who help her meet her goal of reaching the *Bridge of the Gods*. The setbacks are more than she expects, but she trusts the experienced guides she meets along the way, and her story is one of overcoming the biggest challenges in life by pure perseverance. When she finally meets her goal, she says, "Thank you. Not just for the long walk, but for everything the trail had taught me and everything I couldn't yet know, though I felt it somehow contained within me" (Strayed, p. 310).

Everyone who begins a journey of self-discovery to test their physical or intellectual endurance feels afraid, unsure if their abilities can meet the challenges ahead. Some people may be arrogant to believe that this degree is not hard and that they are more than brilliant enough to pull it off. Those people are outliers or are lying to everyone, including themselves. I put up a plaque I found in a store right in front of my writing desk: "Endurance: Through endurance and the encouragement of scriptures, we have hope (Romans 15:4)." I believe my faith carried me through the tough days, the days of feeling like I was an imposter or just too tired to write another sentence or read another research article. My golden retriever, Grace, was my office buddy and biggest encourager on the "I can't do this" and crying-on-my-keyboard days. I dedicated the final dissertation to her, my loving husband, and my great university professors.

You, like Cheryl Strayed (2013), will need emotional support along the way. You cannot do this alone. You must find the strength to endure and persevere even if you doubt this journey you have started. Deciding to take on the challenge of a doctorate takes commitment and sacrifice from you, your family, your colleagues, and your supervisor. Most doctoral students are in demanding full-time jobs. Therefore, before you go any further, you should have a serious talk with your family, supervisors, and coworkers. They need to know when you must complete this undertaking and how they can support you. Classes are only a part of your commitment throughout this endeavor. From the beginning, you will be researching and writing about your topic. If time management is a weakness, it is time to develop that muscle. Remember that the doctorate is a test of persistence and discipline. It would help if you considered that other than class time, you would devote an average of three to six hours a week to classwork and research. Preparing yourself for the time, work, and effort is something you do before starting the degree, not when the world comes crashing down on you. Doctoral students have babies, divorces, job changes and experience deaths in their families during this process. One student discovered she had cancer during her second year in the program. Despite the hellish cancer treatments and overwhelming stress, she was determined to finish her degree. She became one of our biggest success stories. Never had I seen so many weeping faculty members as she crossed the stage to receive her diploma.

> **SNAPSHOT** 📷
>
> Near the end of the second year of my EdD program, my father died of complications from myelodysplastic syndrome. It was spring, and he had just turned 66. I was 41 and wondered how I might live another 40 years in a world where he is not. The disease, like some hateful, shadowy thing coming from underground, had been silent until it was too late. The summer prior, he'd fallen ill with what doctors diagnosed as colitis, and as MDS is very rare, they missed its insidious presence deep in his bone marrow. A November biopsy finally unmasked its horrific face, but by then, he'd lost over 100 pounds. That winter, I researched MDS through Thanksgiving and Christmas as my father became more and more of a ghost. In the

cold dark of January and February, my mother and sister took him for bi-weekly blood transfusions while I sat at a computer, tabs open across the top reading "constructivist assessments" and "MDS life expectancy." Phone calls became rounds of "Mama, I can quit" and "No, you can't."

When the ambulance came for him, eyes open but otherwise unresponsive, in the early hours of April 11, 2023, I was holding him in my arms. We'd been trying unsuccessfully to put his shirt on. I held him against my chest, whispering, "Please don't be scared, Daddy. I'm right here." Not quite two days later, in the deepest quiet shortly before midnight, he drew his last breath in the presence of his wife and children. In the fever dream days that followed, as my family arranged to honor his life, I sat in his chair with my laptop and wrote his obituary, his eulogy, and a midterm paper for my class in gender studies.

One of the last things Daddy said to me was, "I hate that I'll miss your graduation." I remember thinking, "When the earth soon swallows him, how will it not take with him everything else, including me?" During this season of grief, I've considered pausing, or stopping, the pursuit of my degree many times. But then I think of how my father cried on the phone when I called to tell him I'd been accepted to the program. I'm a first-generation college graduate on both sides; every threshold I cross marks the fulfillment of generational sacrifice and lights a path forward for my sisters' children, my cousins' children.

My father, Cecil Grooms, was the smartest man I knew. The qualities I'll need to call on to finish my degree are my inheritance from him, my success a part of his legacy. The road ahead seems long, and I am tired. Thankfully, I've enjoyed the blessing of empathetic professors who've endlessly offered me grace. When this is done and my name is called, my greatest wish is that I will feel the presence of my father. These days, I carry on by picturing that moment, of how I know he'll be there, so close as if to touch me again.

—Kristi Grooms, EdD

TIME MANAGEMENT

We are busy juggling work, family, organization, and exercise routines. Your studies will require papers and presentations for the classes and keeping up with your research reading and writing. At most, you will take six to nine hours a semester. Universities have specific standards for measuring how much time per credit hour the course activities and assignments should take per semester. These are called Carnegie Hours.

> The Carnegie Unit defines a semester unit of credit as equal to a minimum of three hours of work per week for a semester. This schoolwork schedule means that one unit of credit equals three hours of student work per week (1-hour lecture plus 2 hours of homework or 3 hours of lab) for 15 weeks.
>
> (Albright University, 2015, p. 1)

For a three-hour class, the faculty must document 45 instructional, including anything the faculty are supervising, is measurable, directly related to the objectives or course outcomes, or equivalent to activities conducted during direct instructional time. This time could include online discussion boards, videos of lectures, online journals, library research, or final projects (*instructional-equivalencies-chart-carnegie-units-updated-9–22–15.pdf (albright.edu)*). Depending on the program, you will typically take six to nine hours per semester. This accreditation rule should estimate how much time you will be devoting to reading and writing per week, per course.

If you do not create a routine and schedule for writing and studying, you will add incredible stress to your life. The worst thing you can do is to come to class unprepared. Every faculty member can identify students who come in "cold" and think they can fake their knowledge of the assigned readings. Nothing is more stressful than hoping a professor does not call on you to respond to the assigned reading.

4 Credit Course	4 units x 15 weeks	60 instructional hours
3 Credit Course	3 units x 15 weeks	45 instructional hours
4 Credit Online Course		60 Instructional hours need to be charted

Figure 4.1 Carnegie Units.

SNAPSHOT

I posted on my syllabus when students would be expected to present their article critique to the class. I reminded students two weeks before the due date which week they would share their presentation. I also posted the names of the presenters on Blackboard. At the beginning of the first day of presentations, I called out the order of students who would be presenting. One student looked at me in shock. "I'm presenting today?" "Yes, I have told you multiple times this semester." He asked if he could trade places with another student in the lineup. He sat in the back of the room, typing frantically, while the other students presented their critiques. He came up to present and spent 20 minutes reading his slides, never engaging his audience. Based on the assignment's rubric, he scored very low. When he got his feedback and poor grade, he was shocked. He thought he did a great job faking his knowledge of the article. He ended up with a B– in the class.

—anonymous professor

Most of your assignments are written essays or research. Rarely will you experience multiple-choice tests where you must memorize many facts. Occasionally, you may get a quiz, especially in statistics or some legal case studies, but for the most part, you will spend your time reading and writing.

SNAPSHOT

I had a professor who had us read eight leadership books, including his textbook, and he gave 130 multiple-choice questions with three essay questions with a three-hour time frame for completion. It was awful! I almost dropped out of the program and was grateful for a B in the class. He was the only professor who ever did that kind of test, thank goodness.

Time management also means turning in assignments on time. Late assignments are unacceptable. Your reputation and professionalism are based on turning in quality work during the expected timeline. You can only use the excuse of a busy work schedule or sick kids a few times. You are spending a significant amount of money on this degree, which is wasted if you fail the class because of poor time management. Be proactive before you start your program. Ensure you schedule family, exercise, work, and most importantly, sleep time. You lower your chances of success if you are not healthy physically, mentally, and in your relationships. Sometimes you may have to miss vacations or holiday celebrations because you have classwork or research to complete. This need for time and space is essential when you begin your research. Once you finish your course requirements, you enter a period solely working on dissertation research. You are on your clock from there on. Universities expect you to be officially enrolled as you work on your research. That means tuition money every semester. The sooner you finish the paper, the less money you will spend. Sacrifices must be made, but only for a few years.

SNAPSHOT

My doctoral journey was a roller coaster—as most tend to be. Initially, I applied to five large schools and did not get accepted to any of them. I trusted God would lead me to the right place at the right time. A year later, I applied to a smaller school and was accepted. It ended up being a significantly better time for me personally and professionally, even if I could not see it when I originally received five rejection letters. On-campus was the best modality for me based on my learning style, and little did I know, my classmates became my family. Due to COVID restrictions, we were not allowed to meet in person temporarily, and it was like a family reunion when we were able to see each other again. We shared life together—celebrated promotions, babies, and graduations, grieved losses of loved ones, unmet expectations, and lost job opportunities. Professionally, I am grateful for the ability to work for flexible supervisors while earning my degree. They were willing to let me come into the office early so I could leave early to get to classes. I also had an amazing mentor who would remind me that it was acceptable to take a day off work either for my own mental health or to spend a day focused on schoolwork when I was overwhelmed or behind. Personally, my husband and my mom were extremely supportive during the years of earning my degree. During the first year of my doctoral program, I changed jobs, unexpectedly got pregnant, the world shut down for COVID, I miscarried, and I lost a very close friend. During my second year, I got pregnant again, moved across town, and defended my dissertation proposal. During my third year, I had our baby while finishing my dissertation and then defended my final dissertation in time to graduate. Life does not stop because you are working toward a degree. I could not have done this journey without the support of my husband, who encouraged me to apply, believed that I could earn my doctorate, and was essentially a solo parent for the first nine months of our son's life while I finished my degree. My husband also helped me find a rhythm that worked for our family, and we reallocated finances so we could outsource some tasks that were time-consuming and overwhelming (namely, laundry). Looking back, my expectations of career opportunities when starting my degree were unrealistic—graduating and being offered a full-time teaching faculty position at a university the next day. However, the reality was that I applied to multiple schools and various companies, did not receive any feedback from any colleges or universities, interviewed with one company, did not feel it was the right fit, so ended up staying in my same position. A year after graduation, I am looking forward to potential career advancements that my degree will allow me in the future.

—Tia Caster, EdD

WORK AREA AND SUPPLIES

One of the recommendations for all doctoral students is to set up a study/work area in their houses. Find a place in your house that is your designated office. This spot needs a desk, light, and areas for books and papers. Go to an office supply store and get sticky pads, binders, highlighters, or anything else you can think of as part of your study/writing routines. This room or place should be somewhere other than something that interferes with homelife, such as the dining room or bedroom. Choose a spot without any distractions. Avoid using the dining room as your workspace. Any holiday meal could disrupt the organization of your work. It should be somewhere other than where young hands can move papers or draw on your materials. You want a place designated for assignments, not play. Your bedroom may not be the best place to work in if you are married or in a committed relationship. Your partner may want to sleep while you want to work. Be careful if you use your office at work. People lose focus on their doctoral assignments and begin thinking about work deadlines and problems. Granted, you know how to focus on a large project, so rely on the tried-and-true habits you have gained through your previous experience. Be mindful that using your work computer for a personal endeavor may violate some workplace policies. Then, once you get your space, make a sign. Post "I am writing" on your door or something. Teach your family that when this sign is on the door, you are not to be disturbed unless the house is on fire, someone is dying, or you win the lottery. If you have your family's support, they should respect the time and space you need.

Investing in good writing software for your computer and learning multiple ways to save and store your work are also essential. If you have a flash drive for your work, buy another one. You want to make sure doctoral assignments and work are clear. There are websites where you can save your work in the Cloud, so if something happens to your flash drive or computer, you have your work in a place where it is safe. Again, it is not recommended that you use your workplace Cloud storage. If you leave that position, will you lose your work? Do not take that chance. The stories of students losing their paper by fire, computer theft, or flash drive are too numerous to count. One of my study partners had her purse stolen while loading groceries in a big-box store parking lot. Her only flash drive was in her bag, and she lost all her work. Do not think it cannot happen to you. It is common to experience nightmares of losing your hard work and having to start over.

SELF-CARE

How do you manage your stress? It is a given that you will be stressed during this process. Stress is like adding rocks to a backpack as you are walking uphill. The more you add, the more you slow down and sometimes quit because you are overwhelmed or just tired of the weight. Before you begin this journey, you need to come up with a plan to deal with stressful situations. Coping strategies can be positive or negative. Which of the following coping strategies do you use when you feel overwhelmed?

Avoiding conversations with others	Gardening	
Binge-watching TV	Hiding from everyone	
Biting your fingernails	Making lists	
Caffeine	Mediating	
Cleaning house or car	Playing online games	
Criticizing yourself	Praying or Going to Church	
Cycling	Procrastinating assignments	
Dancing	Shopping	
Drinking Alcohol	Singing	
Drinking Energy Drinks	Sleeping too much or too litle	
Drinking soft drinks	Smoking	
Driving fast	Taking a bath or shower	
Eating candy	Talking to counselor or confident	
Eating fast-food	Using Recreational or Prescription drugs	
Eating too much or too litle	Walking/running	
Escaping into social media	Writing in a journal	
Exercising	Yoga	
Fighting with loved ones	Other	

Figure 4.2 Coping strategies during stressful times.

You can identify positive and negative coping strategies for addressing stressful seasons.

Unfortunately, we develop habits that are not always the best for us. Faculty in doctoral programs have reported seeing students gain weight, become depressed, have marriage problems, and sometimes lose their jobs due to the overwhelming feeling of carrying too much work. People get sick with migraines and stomach issues. You spend much of your time sitting in front of a computer or reading research. Time passes, and then you realize you have not gotten up in hours. Sedentary life is not suitable for you. Before you start this program, create a healthy plan for addressing your stress.

There are a variety of apps that can help monitor your exercise and eating patterns. Pack your lunch and dinner instead of stopping for fast food, and watch your caffeine intake. Get up and walk around. All these pieces of advice you have heard a million times, but you do want to survive this journey without mental, emotional, and physical issues arising to slow you from reaching your goals.

SUMMARY

Much of the success of this degree journey is based on how well you prepare before you start. Recognizing your strengths and weaknesses can be the first step in planning for personal remediation. Creating a space for work, creating time management routines, and taking care of yourself mentally and physically are essential for survival.

TRAVEL JOURNAL

- How do your family and friends feel about you starting a doctoral program? How is this support connected to your self-efficacy in completing the journey?
- How do you set up your schedule when you have deadlines?
- What positive self-care habits can you start before you begin this degree to ensure that you arrive at your destination (graduation day) healthy and happy?
- Who is your accountability person to help you stay on track on the personal goals you are creating?

PACKING CHECKLIST

- Create a space for your college work.
- Find appropriate Cloud space to store your assignments.
- Consider how you cope with stress, and create a plan to maintain your emotional and physical health during the program.

REFERENCES

Albright University. (2015). *Instructional equivalencies chart.* Retrieved from instructional-equivalencies-chart-carnegie-units-updated-9-22-15.pdf (albright.edu)

Strayed, C. (2013). *Wild: Lost to found on the pacific crest trail.* Vintage Books.

Part III

Avoiding Quicksand on the Trail

Chapter 5

The Big Three
Classes, Comprehensive Exams, and Capstone Projects

CHAPTER OBJECTIVES

- Recognize the three main components of a doctoral program.
- Prepare for written assignments.
- Examine the process for comprehensive exam preparation and procedures.
- Explore the different types of capstone projects in a doctoral program.

INTRODUCTION

In hiking vocabulary, the *big three* refer to the three most essential items you need on the trail: a sleeping bag, tent, and backpack. Here we refer to the big three as the three components of a doctoral program. You must accomplish all three to make it to the end of this journey with a diploma. The big three are classes, comprehensive exams, and capstone projects. This chapter will outline the big three so you can plan your journey with the right gear in mind.

NUMBER 1: CLASSES AND ASSIGNMENTS

Attending your classes is crucially important. That is probably a strange statement; you will attend classes. It is incredible how many people do not attend class or come in late and expect the faculty or other students to help them with the information they miss. Each course is progressively connected to your research. Your faculty should provide as much information as possible to help you complete a thesis based on research-based theory and practice. You must attend class to get the essential knowledge and skills. Doctoral programs typically do not allow students to make lower than a B in any class; attendance may be calculated as part of the final grade. Coming in late is also considered distracting to the other students and the faculty. We all understand traffic and last-minute work issues, but you must try to be in class on time as much as possible. If you feel your job or family obligations are too demanding to attend class or turn in your assignments dependably, consider undertaking this degree during another season, when you have more time. There is no judgment here. The time for this work is when you can focus on it without guilt or condemnation.

Once you have an idea of your topic of study (read how to pick this in an upcoming chapter), base as many of your assignments on that topic as you can. This way, you can use these assignments to boost your knowledge of your topic from many different viewpoints. For example, the concepts you learn in a program evaluation course may guide you in evaluating a program associated with your topic. Every class may open a new dimension to your research you may not have considered before. The papers could be added to your literature review only if it does not contain your opinion. Personal opinions have no place in the research.

During the first few meetings for your classes, meet the other students and build relationships. Networking with other doctoral students helps you in many ways. If you connect with a group of four or five students, they can be your study group for future assignments. Everyone's expertise can help the collective group be successful. For example, one person is very good at creating PowerPoint presentations. Another student is adept at research design and methodology, and another is a great presenter; cooperative learning helps the whole group increase its prospects of getting a good grade. As time passes, you learn to trust each other to get through all challenges together. One group, for instance, had one person who posted all the assignment deadlines and shared the calendar with her group. As a direct result, no one turned in anything late, which, in turn, relieved much stress. Your group could also study together for exams. It is incredible how much you will depend upon each other for encouragement to finish. Finally, you are networking with people in education who can connect you to future career opportunities. The world of education is constantly changing, and after you complete this doctorate, you will be qualified to seek jobs that allow you to use your new knowledge and skills. With that said, your professional reputation will be shown during your classes by how you interact with the faculty and other students. If you are a team player and supportive person, people will think of you when a position is open in their organization. However, if you whine, complain, and are confrontational, good luck finding people who will recommend you for the big jobs.

> **SNAPSHOT** 📷
>
> Since my doctoral program was asynchronous, a number of my professors employed a dialectical approach to learning through required discussion board posts and

> responses. At first, I assumed it was busy work. Our professors were active participants, though, reading and responding to almost everything my cohort wrote on those boards. I found these discussions to be an invaluable source of knowledge. I could see how our different perceptions of the content were shaped by our individual experiences; reading these and reflecting on them deepened my understanding of the readings and helped me see more connections between the text and my own dissertation in progress.

Planning Your Writing Assignments

Since writing assignments is the norm for this graduate degree level, it is highly recommended that you assess your writing skills and strategies developed in academia or a professional setting over the past years. What type of writer are you? Torrance et al. (1994) identified three types of writing processes for students in higher education, representing planners, revisers, and mixed-strategy. In their study, they wanted to discover when and how graduate students planned and wrote their writing assignments. They narrowed down to two factors: when students wanted to make content and structure changes and the number of drafts of a paper they revised before submission. The *planners* focused on the "think and then write" strategy. They tended to take notes, develop mind maps, and organize notes before writing drafts and revising. They averaged two drafts of a text before submission. The *revisers* were hit-and-miss in their processes since they tended to write and then go back and revise. They could be described as think-while-you-write writers. Overall, the research by Torrance et al. (1994) showed that this method of planning and writing was slow and ineffective. Finally, the mixed-strategy writer planned their writing by brainstorming, taking notes, using mind maps, making an outline before writing a draft, and then revising. This process seemed to show the most success for academic writers in completing writing assignments with better quality. Rudd (1984) contends that failure in a doctoral program is linked to students with a slow writing process that could discourage them from having a positive experience developing their research papers. It is not that these writers are incapable of creating valid research; the writing of this research bogs them down and, therefore, creates a barrier to completion.

If you have anxiety when facing a writing assignment, some courses at universities and junior colleges can help you develop this skill. For some of you, that might be your first stop before applying for a doctoral degree. The more you write, get feedback, and revise, the more you will improve and become more confident in the writing process.

NUMBER 2: COMPREHENSIVE EXAMS

Almost all doctoral programs require some end-of-program comprehensive exam. These exams are written, oral, or both. These are usually written essays that expect you to synthesize and apply all the concepts from the courses you took during the degree. The exam could be written at home or, most likely, on campus. It is a full day or two days of 4–6 hours of writing responses to essay questions. It can be overwhelming and stressful if you are not prepared. Each program is different in any case. Some programs expect students to take state or national professional certification exams instead of written comps if the program goals are connected to certification.

Preparing for these comprehensive exams is a lot of work. Keep your syllabi and focus on the course objectives or outcomes. Objectives and outcomes are excellent study guides so you are focused on the possible questions. Keep your papers and reflect on the feedback. Keep your textbooks since your essays are more robust when you can cite the authors you have read, including citing references from lectures. Some students keep spreadsheets of concepts covered in all the classes to use as a study guide. You cannot study for this exam the night or week before it is given. A good study technique is to practice writing essays with a time limit or reading research papers and critiquing the validity of the studies. This process will also be more straightforward if you are a proficient writer. Knowing how to plan and format a paper in a logical sequence is vital. Sentence structure is also essential. In most programs, you cannot graduate or complete your dissertation proposal until you have successfully passed your comprehensive exams.

What if you fail one or more parts of the comprehensive exam? Review the student handbook and the policies for the program. Talk to your advisor if you already know you need help with writing in a structured situation. Sadly, most faculty know who will not survive this hurdle. Students with a history of poor writing and who do not seek support from a writing center will struggle. No one wants you to fail. You spent too much time and money to fail now. Work on your academic writing skills and openly seek tutoring if this is your weakness. You are responsible for your remediation, not the faculty or university.

NUMBER 3: CAPSTONE PROJECTS

The doctoral programs that are accredited include some capstone projects. It is recommended to avoid programs that do not have a capstone project. Some educational institutions will not recognize your advanced degree if there is not some assignment that requires research-applied projects. These projects can be referred to as a culminating or applied inquiry that involves thoroughly searching peer-reviewed studies that expand your worldview. The goal of these projects is to teach you to follow a scientific model of inquiry. While these projects are very time-consuming and challenging, the hope is that after you finish your degree, you will apply this process when making decisions about organizational changes. Spending limited resources to solve problems in your organization without research is never recommended. Your automatic response to new ideas should always be based on research.

How many organizations have spent millions of dollars on a product or program in hopes of significantly improving student achievement, only to find out later that it was a waste of time and money? Most universities require capstone projects that can be a traditional dissertation or dissertation in practice (DiP).

Dissertation in Practice (DiP)

A DiP is an action research where students must find a problem in practice in their organization or school district. Action research is a common type of research that requires an assessment of a problem, creating an action, evaluating the action, and reflecting on the results. The goal is to find solutions for issues arising in education. Most DiPs are in EdD programs since they are practitioner's degrees. The goal of action research is to find practical solutions through the lens of theories and reflections. *Action research* is a pragmatic process combining practical and scientific methods to solve situations directly affecting the researcher and their organization (Mertler, 2019). Innovation is a significant part of action research. Thinking outside the box and testing improvement methods in education systems keep our field so dynamic. You can find examples of outstanding DiPs on the Carnegie Project on the Education Doctorate (CPED) Resource Center.

The process for creating a DiP varies from university to university, but most have the following sequence:

1. Identify an issue affecting your organization, school district, or school.
2. Research your topic.
3. Draft a proposal of an action plan.
4. Defend the proposal in a formal presentation in front of your faculty committee.
5. Apply the action plan, evaluate results, and report results.

Some universities allow small collaborative groups of students to work on the DiP, but do not be surprised if you are alone.

There are pitfalls to group projects, such as people dropping out of the program. The best programs have policies and procedures to circumvent these situations.

Traditional Dissertation

A traditional dissertation only sometimes involves problem-solving but is more about explaining a phenomenon. A DiP centers on the "how," and a dissertation focuses on the "why" or "what." "A dissertation is a formal document demonstrating your ability to conduct research that makes an original contrition to theory or practice" (Roberts et al., 2019, p. 29). The traditional dissertation is broken into five chapters that we will review more in-depth in future chapters. Most PhD programs in education require traditional dissertations as the capstone project. The dissertation is a solo endeavor; however, if you choose the right faculty members to sponsor or support your research, you are not alone. The problem is that students may overly depend on their faculty advisors or not include them in any part of the research planning. Both ends of this spectrum spell disaster for a successful dissertation. There is a healthy balance when working with your faculty advisors. Remember, they have already completed a dissertation, so they know firsthand what you are experiencing. They have ways of softening the process so you will feel confident in your research.

If you complete your classes and pass your comprehensive exams, you are only partially finished with your degree. Without completing and getting full approval for your capstone project, you are considered "all but dissertation" (ABD).

Programs designate research courses primarily for you to complete your research. These courses keep you fully enrolled and paying tuition until you finish your project. The timeline is up to you. People typically take two to four years to complete their capstone project, and some of that work coincides with your courses. It is not uncommon for people to take longer. If you take a leave of absence, there are consequences. You may lose focus, or your topic may become obsolete. You may lose your committee members and chairperson if they leave the university. If this degree is essential to you, finish what you start.

Encouragement and recommendations from students who have come before you:

- *If a program starts with a cohort, I will give it high priority.*
- *After deciding who you would like to be your dissertation chair, talk to them about professors they work well with. I have seen professors delay dissertation progress because they had conflicts with each other—no one has time for that.*
- *Be sure to celebrate the milestones of the journey.*
- *Hire a good editor.*
- *Don't give up. Take a break if you must, but don't give up.*
- *If you have difficulty doing classwork at home, go to the library, where there is fewer distraction.*
- *Read your dissertation chair and dissertation committee's dissertations.*
- *"Treat yourself often." (Kelley)*
- *"There are many recommendations I would give to anyone pursuing their doctoral degree: self-discipline, goal-setting, note-taking, time management, etc., but the greatest one would be for a student to prepare to write, and write a lot, with all things entailed in the writing process (write, revise, edit, rewrite, peer-review, and so on). Even if you feel you are a good writer, be prepared to have your writing*

criticized and even rejected at times, but no matter what . . . write, write, write. And when you think you are done . . . write some more." (Gregory)
- *"One recommendation that I have for doctoral students is to focus on the goal of attaining the doctoral degree, and don't fight the system, even when you know in your heart you are doing the right thing. There will be many opportunities to publish once you have been awarded the degree. Secondly, the doctoral journey is incredibly lonely, so be certain to take care of yourself and spend time away from your studies with loved ones, friends, and peers. Lastly, when you feel like quitting, don't. Seek out support, talk to your friends and family, and communicate with your committee members, who, if they are worthy of serving on a doctoral committee, will encourage you and help you get on the right path toward degree achievement. If you don't have a committee chair or committee members that you can work with and sincerely take an interest in your success, contact the institution, and seek out a new team. (Tony)*

SUMMARY

Aspiring doctoral students need to know that this degree is not just about attending classes and doing homework. You will learn concepts that expand your topic beyond the surface level you have on your mind. Taking the comprehensive exams is not a punishment but a method that allows you to apply all the knowledge you have gained in your classes to various real-world scenarios. The capstone project is the most significant difference between a student who is ABD and a person who graduates. Going to classes and using the information from those classes add dimension to your research. You end up quoting experts in the field you were unaware of when you started this journey. You begin to think, write, and talk like a scholar.

A doctorate program's components are designed to give you the power to have an idea and promote it scientifically and convincingly.

TRAVEL JOURNAL
- You have decided to return to school as an adult. What are you hoping to gain personally and professionally from the courses you take during this program?
- Test anxiety is a real issue for many adults. How do you overcome feeling unprepared when evaluated on your knowledge and skills?
- What type of research is dissertation in practice or dissertation connected with your professional aspirations? Why does one of these capstone assignments connect with your career plan?

> **PACKING CHECKLIST**
> - Plan how you will organize your books, papers, and research in preparation for the comprehensive exams.
> - Align as much of your homework to your research topic as possible.
> - Build relationships with other doctoral students to create a network of scholars.

REFERENCES

Mertler, C. (2019). *The Wiley handbook of action research in education.* John Wiley & Sons, Incorporated.

Roberts, C., & Hyatt, L. (2019). *The dissertation journey: A practical and comprehensive guide to planning, writing, and defending your dissertation* (3rd ed.). Corwin.

Rudd, E. (1984). Research in postgraduate education. *Higher Education Research and Development, 3*, 109–120.

Torrance, M., Thomas, G. V., & Robinson, E. J. (1994). The writing strategies of graduate research students in the social sciences. *Higher Education, 27*(3), 379–392. https://doi.org/10.1007/BF03179901

Chapter 6
Rules of the Road

CHAPTER OBJECTIVES

- Review and understand the responsibilities of students in a doctoral program.
- Explore university policies concerning late assignments, tuition, continuous enrollment, plagiarism, and using artificial intelligence.
- Distinguish university systems for complaints against faculty or the program.

INTRODUCTION

Before any trip to a foreign country, wise people research that country's laws. There are many people in foreign prisons who did not think the local country's laws applied to them. The point is that every university has published policies on the website, in the university catalog, and in program-specific handbooks. Program and university leaders tend to go overboard in communicating what is acceptable and what will not be tolerated. These policy manuals over-communicate the rules since many students before you challenged the rules and either won or lost their complaints. University leadership learns from each experience to clarify the details of policies more and more in hopes of avoiding future litigation. Remember, institutions of higher education share information with each other and use this information to expand their protections from lawsuits.

Before we go further into the scope of university policies, please remember that this book reviews the generalities of doctoral programs, and you cannot use this information against the university you are attending if you fall into a situation where you broke a rule. You are responsible for reading the program's handbooks, policies, and syllabus. No one ever wins by saying, "Well, I didn't know there was a rule about that . . ." *Ignorantia juris non excusat*—ignorance of the law excuses no one.

SYLLABUS

A *syllabus* is a contract between the faculty member/university and the student. Again, due to litigations, the length of syllabi has increased to include policies and expectations. Examples of topics covered in syllabi include attendance, assignment expectations, due dates, penalties for late work, and plagiarism. Some students read the assignment outline or the actual assignment descriptions. If you do not read carefully, you may find that you are missing key details of the class that make a difference between passing or failing. Review the assignment rubrics on the syllabus or the course Blackboard or Canvas site before starting an assignment. It is incredible how many students do not read the rubric and wonder why they earn a low score.

ATTENDANCE

Attendance rules vary among universities. Some have tight 25% rules, meaning, you cannot miss more than 25% of the class meetings. Accredited programs ensure that classes meet a specific amount of time each semester with coursework included. If you are late or absent, you may have faculty that deducts points from your final grade. At some universities, you will fail the course if you miss too many classes or are late too many times. Of course, there are faculty who do not care about attendance at all. Whether you are there or not, it is your dime and your responsibility for the information taught in the class. The attendance requirements are questions you should ask the admission committee during your interview. Suppose you are in a season when there is no guarantee that you can be in class on time each week due to family or professional demands. In that case, you should reconsider the degree until you meet attendance expectations.

There was a professor who had taught this one course for over 15 years. His slides for his lecture were never updated in all that time, but that did not stop him from lecturing for three hours straight as if everything he said were current and highly reliable. If people asked questions, he would pause and answer the questions. However, he stopped when class time was up, even if he had not finished the lecture. If he finished early, he would repeat the whole lecture from the beginning so the class would end on time. One night, a student was held up at work and walked in 30 minutes late. The professor told the student to speak to him after class.

After everyone had left, the professor pulled out his slides and lectured the late student to make up for the 30 minutes he missed. That situation is not normal, so if you are late, try to get the notes from others. Not all faculty post their lectures for students to use to study, so they may not be available. Be on time and go to class. It is respectful and professional behavior.

LATE ASSIGNMENTS

One of the most significant pet peeves faculty have with students is late work. Oddly, since most students in education doctoral programs are teachers or school leaders, it is ironic how many turn in late work for various reasons. Most assignments are now uploaded to learning management systems like Blackboard or Canvas.

These systems are used for grading, uploading course materials, discussion boards, and communications between students and faculty. Most faculty do not want hard copies of papers but choose to have students upload assignments. There may be very tight timelines for completing the assignments, such as Thursday by 11:58 p.m. Once a student is late, the learning management system flags the assignment. Some faculty take off points for late work. Late work indicates that a student needs to be more organized. The syllabus is specific about when assignments are due, so there are no surprises. Students have given excuses like family gatherings, sick kids, personal illness, or work excuses. All these are acceptable if a faculty member gives grace. Refrain from counting on everyone being understanding. Faculty have grade deadlines at midterm and finals. They do not like to be late either. It can cause issues with their job status.

If you have no choice for turning in a late assignment, contact the faculty member as soon as the issue arises, and pray they understand. Do not avoid turning in the assignment at all and then expect grace or not expect a failing grade. An online student did not turn in assignments for the first four weeks of an eight-week session. On week 5, he turned in seven late and poorly done assignments. He was amazed that the faculty member gave him straight zeroes for everything. The faculty member said, "I have a life too. I plan out my grading schedule each week. I am not adding on seven more papers to grade just because you were unorganized."

TUITION

This degree is expensive, and there are avenues to pay for it with financial support or in installments. You do have to keep up with your bills. Universities are businesses, and they have expenses that tuition revenue covers. Pay your tuition and fees on time to avoid being blocked out of classes or even dropped from the university. If you are dropped, you still owe the university for your courses. Getting upset when you get a late payment notice and screaming at the cashier will not change anyone's mind to help you. However, you have some wiggle room if you are on a scholarship and that deposit is late. Go to the finance office to work out payment plans or ask them to help you get financial aid. You are working so hard; quitting after a few semesters would be a waste of time and money.

CONTINUOUS ENROLLMENT

Some doctoral programs front-load all courses and only allow students to begin their capstone projects (dissertation or dissertation in practice) once all courses are completed and you have completed your comprehensive exams. Some programs allow you to work on your project while you take courses. In either case, you must be enrolled in "dissertation" or "research" courses while you work on your project, whether you are taking content courses or not. These are usually one-hour courses, but tuition is attached to the time you work with faculty on your project. It would be best if you continued to enroll as a full-time student while working on your research. The time you take to complete this project is up to you.

If you procrastinate, you will pay more money. You also take the chance that your faculty advisor ignores you if you are not making progress on your research; they may not prioritize you over students working and communicating with them. You should not expect faculty advisors to call or email you every week to remind you to do your work. The best advice is to stay focused, do the work, and get it done within your set timeline.

COMPLAINTS ABOUT FACULTY

It would be wonderful if all faculty were easygoing, positive people who give fantastic lectures and give students outstanding support all the time. Most of the faculty you will meet are great teachers and researchers. However, like anywhere else in the working world, some not-so-great teachers and researchers exist. You can file a complaint if you genuinely feel a faculty member has treated you poorly, unethically, or unfairly. The chain of command is a process that all education institutions enforce. The recommendation is that you first speak to the faculty member. Try to work out the issue with them before going over their head. The relationship between students and faculty is fragile, so only rock the boat if you cannot work it out with them first. If the issue still needs to be resolved at this level, you can go to the department chair, the assistant dean, the dean (in that order), and then the VP of academics before jumping to the president or board of trustees. Your university may have another pecking order when trouble arises, so check your student handbook or catalog for the process for filing a complaint. You will be asked to prove malfeasance. Did this faculty member purposefully mistreat you for not following university policies? Most universities give faculty members the benefit of the doubt, so build your case with facts, not emotions or rumors. Connect your complaint with concise evidence, including a timeline. Ensure your letter is free from spelling and grammar errors, especially if you contest a grade.

If you are being harassed in any way by a faculty member or any university employee, jump to the department chair or dean right away. Again, you should have clear evidence to prove your case. Universities have severe consequences for faculty or staff that act inappropriately with students.

My husband loves to tell the story about his time as a graduate student when he tried to meet with his professor about a grade. He began showing the professor his paper to show where the grade was wrong, and the professor yelled and threw the book at him. Luckily, the book hit the doorframe instead of my husband's head. That is an extreme, and you will not have that experience.

PLAGIARISM

The thought of unintentionally plagiarizing material in a manuscript makes most researchers cringe in fear. The APA 7th edition manual states, "There are two common types of plagiarism: (a) improper use of someone else's words and (b) improper use of someone else's ideas. Both forms of plagiarism involve using someone else's words or ideas without appropriately acknowledging the author or source" (p. 246). Be careful. Cite whenever you use information from another author. Check your APA guide for the correct format. You can always cite. Give credit to those who work or the ideas you used. Quotation marks for the use of exact words. If you paraphrase, that is, summarize, rearrange, or change the wording, you need to credit the source (American Psychological Association, 2020). References include information you get from Internet sites. Therefore, being organized with your articles and books is essential. It is easy to be caught up in your writing and forget to cite the ideas you gained from other authors.

It cannot be overstressed that plagiarism is serious. It can ruin your university experience and possible future career. For example, a popular district leader should have reacted appropriately to an accusation during a public meeting. A disgruntled community member decided this was his opportunity to attack the leader by sending the leader's dissertation to an editor, and some paragraphs were designated as plagiarized. The leader needed to do an adequate job rephrasing quotations and citing well. This report was made public, and the community was appalled. The university where he earned his degree opened an investigation, and the result could have been better. The leader's university doctorate was retracted, and he resigned in humiliation. He lost his reputation and future because he was careless with his writing. Because plagiarism has become a common issue, especially with the rise of artificial intelligence (AI), universities now use unique online systems that can detect plagiarism. Students may also have access to these systems to check their papers before turning them in for a grade. It is common for someone to plagiarize, so using tools available online unintentionally can be helpful. Many universities publish your dissertation of practice or dissertations, which are available worldwide to read. Do not gamble on your future by taking shortcuts.

ARTIFICIAL INTELLIGENCE (AI)

The use of artificial intelligence natural language processing (NLP) in academic writing is a new phenomenon storming the gates of higher education institutions. Using AI to generate writing for research or any assignment is not allowed. However, with companies like Google, Microsoft, and NVIDIA creating text about any topic, the temptation to use this new technology as a shortcut is unethical and will not be tolerated. Again, universities are using plagiarism-detecting software such as Turnitin to help curb violations. Academic journals are developing stringent policies concerning the use of NLP for submissions. While using spell- or grammar-checking software is acceptable, the expectation is that the content of the written research or assignments is original.

ACADEMIC INTEGRITY VIOLATIONS AND APPEALS

Nothing blocks your higher education experience more than violating academic integrity. The International Center for Academic Integrity (ICAI, 2021) "defines academic integrity as a commitment to six fundamental values: honesty, trust, fairness, respect, responsibility, and courage" (p. 6). The core of this concept is to give authors of publications and ideas credit for the work they have written. Cheating destroys your credibility and the creditability of the university you are attending. Not very many people take the chance, but some students take shortcuts and gamble so that no one catches them.

While faculty members are busy people grading a lot of student work, they are savvy in detecting when someone is cheating. Read the student handbook to understand what a violation of academic integrity is at your university. If cheating is discovered, the faculty member will confront the student to find the reasons for the transgression. They must meet with the student quickly and ascertain whether this infraction was done intentionally.

Most universities require the faculty member to report any academic integrity violations to the registrar, the vice president of academics, and the dean of the college within a couple of days. Each university has its timeline. Some universities have an academic integrity committee of faculty members to review cases and make a ruling. Students will get a notification by email or mail stating the steps they must take to defend their actions. Two things can happen if they are found guilty of an academic integrity violation, warning/probation, or expulsion.

Students can appeal the ruling, but they must show that they did not commit a violation or that the faculty member is guilty of malfeasance. The university's senior leaders will review the appeal, but if they deny the appeal, the student is out of options. There is no appeal to the appeal.

SUMMARY

Very few people in doctoral programs break the rules. Sometimes, society focuses on the rule breakers more than those who do the right thing for the right reasons. Like any new journey, you need to be very aware of the campus culture and follow that road's rules. Staying in your lane of ethical behavior will make your experience during this program less stressful and more fulfilling. Read all the handbooks, catalogs, and syllabi carefully to be fully informed and not surprised by bumps in the road.

TRAVEL JOURNAL

- How do you feel about rules? Are they essential for our society, or do they stifle our creativity?
- Do you seek forgiveness rather than permission? How has this choice worked for you in the past?
- How do university policies ensure the quality of your educational experience?
- Was there a time in your life when you were tempted to do something unethical? How did you overcome the temptation?
- How do you respond if you feel you are being treated unfairly? Give an example of a time in your life when you were unfairly treated, and the actions you took.

PACKING CHECKLIST

- Read the program or university handbook of policies.
- Highlight due dates and review carefully all rubrics for your assignments.

REFERENCES

American Psychological Association. (2020). *Publication manual of the American Psychological Association 2020: The official guide to APA style* (7th ed.). American Psychological Association.

International Center for Academic Integrity [ICAI]. (2021). *The fundamental values of academic integrity* (3rd ed.). Retrieved from www.academicintegrity.org/the-fundamental-valuesof-academic-integrity

Part IV
Crossing the Oceans

Chapter 7
Research Expedition

CHAPTER OBJECTIVES

- Determine interesting topics related to your career or career goal.
- Narrow your topic of interest.
- Evaluate the feasibility and relevance of the topic of interest.
- Analyze personal bias and ethical considerations.
- Create a plan to reach the "end" goal of graduation.

INTRODUCTION

Dissertation planning can begin long before the committee is assigned. Determining a topic, considering bias, and creating a plan for your journey are some things to consider in advance. A topic may dominate your thoughts for two or more years. Consider this time much like a research expedition. Investigation, discovery, and exploration are all part of this early process. Spending some time and energy on establishing the topic and understanding your own bias early in the process may assist you as you progress toward the end goal of graduation. Many people finish ABD (all but dissertation) because they get tired of their subject or the research becomes meaningless. This can be prevented, and this chapter will walk you through the process of choosing a topic, narrowing the topic, analyzing the feasibility of the topic, and creating a realistic expectation and plan for research.

CHOOSING A TOPIC

There are a few ways to select your topic. First, what is your interest, passion, or soapbox? Every leader is passionate about one issue plaguing their organization or educational system. Begin there. If you have many ideas (lucky you), begin reading educational journals, such as educational leadership, or go to websites, such as the Wallace Foundation or the Rand Corporation. They have all the current hot topics in education improvement that you can choose. Also, consider your endgame. What do you want to do after you earn this degree? If you want to teach in higher education, your topic should relate to the courses of study you want to teach. If you want a leadership position in your company, think of what expertise may help you achieve that goal. Employers look for experts to lead their companies.

When considering a topic, it should be connected to your career path. Many people walk into the program with an idea to research but it has nothing to do with their professional future. A candidate wanted to research why young drivers like loud cars. He hated the loud noise and wondered if it was connected to young drivers' economic status or education. While this may be an interesting study, his career path was to become a superintendent, so the topic and his career path did not intersect. He ended up researching graduation rates compared to an increase in technology programs in high schools. This was a better match than he could leverage as he began his search for leadership positions. Think about how this research can expand your knowledge so you can find a position that could use that knowledge base. Begin with a broad topic, and narrow it down after reading additional research. You do not want to state the obvious, such as, "Low-income students do not perform as well as more affluent students." This fact is known to be true. What other aspect can you consider within this topic? Your professors will mostly say, "So what?" or "We already know the answer to that question—dig deeper." For a time, transformational leadership was a hot topic. When a student proposed their transformational leadership topic to me, I would point to my bookshelf and show them ten books on the subject. "Tell me something these authors haven't proven already."

Consider one snowflake! Snowflakes are unique; no two are alike. Likewise, your dissertation topic should be distinctive. You should not repeat the exact study that someone else has completed. A dissertation should be unique and expand the research which has been done in the field of interest. In the winter, when you examine a snowflake on your glove, you can see the boundaries of the flake and its distinct shape. Your dissertation topic needs the same type of boundaries. Too often, candidates are captivated by the beauty of the snowy mountain and want to explore broad topics rather than sticking with a single snowflake. This can lead to difficulty in analysis and seemingly meaningless results. In contrast, a dissertation that is focused on a unique, narrow topic allows the researcher to pinpoint results and demonstrate meaningful conclusions. The boundaries of a snowflake help create its distinct beauty, like the distinction of your research topic. So as you consider the dissertation, stay clear of those vast mountain slopes and stick with a snowflake approach.

NARROWING THE TOPIC

Some may struggle to narrow down a topic. During this process, consider asking yourself the following questions: "What data can I gain access to (after IRB approval) that few would have the privilege of gaining?" Is there a population that I can survey or interview that others may not be able to connect with? Is there a dataset that I may be able to gain permission to use that others cannot? Are there participants' stories that need to be heard that only I can hear? If there is data that you can access but others cannot, it may be a good reason to pursue this topic of research.

Another option for narrowing a topic involves finding recent dissertations on a broad topic of interest. If you locate several dissertations of interest and direct your attention to Chapter 5, you may find a section labeled "Future Research." This area will give you an idea of where the doctoral graduate feels that additional research is needed. They have likely spent many hours researching and reading. Often, recent dissertations will give readers a good idea of where more future research is needed. Gathering ten dissertations and checking this section for patterns or similar narrow topics may give you a good idea of a topic that may be of interest to you.

In the end, there are many ways to determine and narrow a topic. Choose a topic about a career interest that is unique and will inspire your perseverance. If you are going to explore and research a topic for years, make sure it is one you want to stick with.

SNAPSHOT

I spent years learning all I could about a content area. In each course through my doctoral program, I invested all my energy into fully understanding a topic. But as I neared the dissertation phase of my program, I was burnt out. Forcing myself to read any more on the topic became impossible, and I simply did not want to research that particular phenomenon. So I was honest with my dissertation chair, and she asked questions and sought to understand where my interests lie and pushed me to change direction. In the end, I pursued a new area of interest for my dissertation topic. Reading and researching a new topic gave me energy and pushed me to accomplish the work necessary to complete the dissertation. My advice would be to allow yourself to change direction if needed! It can be really tough to set aside research or writing when you know how much time you have invested, but in the end, finding joy in the journey, even if it is a winding road, is much more important!

ADDITIONAL CONSIDERATIONS AS YOU EXPLORE THE TOPIC

Now that you have an idea, begin researching your narrowed topic to see how much information you can find on the subject. You can search dissertations written in the past for recommendations or search recent publications from peer-reviewed journals. Brainstorm your topic with your chair, with your study group, or even with a spouse or friend. They may have perspectives you might not have considered or may lead you to additional research of interest to you.

You must also consider how one might design the study of this topic. Can you use archival data to find out the answers to your questions? Can you interview leaders, teachers, students, or parents to find the answers to your questions? Is there a program in your organization with data available that will give you an answer to your questions? Again, if the answer is common knowledge, why do the research? Conversely, if your research is meaningful and unique, you will never stumble when asked why you should do the research.

Another consideration at this stage is whether the data you want to use will be available and accessible. If data is not archival and you will be collecting data from participants, consider the participant. For example, suppose you want confidential data from a vulnerable population (children). In that case, a school district or agency may be unlikely to allow you access to the information (whether it is archival or not). Necessary precautions must be in place if one plans to work with a vulnerable population. It is never too early to begin considering the availability or accessibility of the data that you are interested in attaining.

The creation of a study is like an upside-down pyramid or funnel. Start with a very broad topic and narrow it down to specific objectives (McGregor, 2018). This process can take some time and energy. It may involve discussions with colleagues and extensive reading. In the end, a well-defined and concise topic can lead to a clear problem, decisive research questions, and distinct purpose. So invest the time and energy now, because later, it will make the process easier to navigate.

WHAT IS BIAS RESEARCH?

Choosing and narrowing a topic is important and should not be considered without acknowledging that everyone has bias. Human perceptions about issues are based on personal experiences or what one has been taught. When a doctoral student begins searching for a topic, they tend to gravitate toward topics that make them righteously angry. There is nothing wrong with making this the starting spot for the topic; however, a dissertation is not a venue for airing angry opinions and supporting the point of view with similar narratives. A good

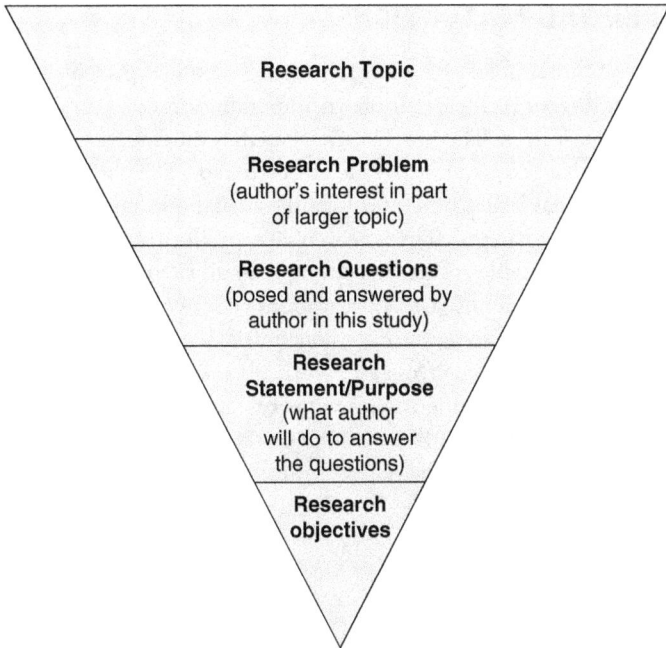

Figure 7.1 McGregor's inverted pyramid.

researcher looks at an issue from all angles, not just the ones that confirm your beliefs or experiences.

Consider this example: a candidate wanted to prove that a program being used in her district was inherently racist and did not allow students of color to graduate. Her committee questioned her perception of the correlation between this program and the dropout rate for students of color. They recognized that there are many factors for low graduation rates for different demographic populations. However, she could not answer their questions. It was her perception, not tied to logic or research, and nothing would dissuade her from her point of view. She was asked by her committee to research the program and how it was performing in other school districts throughout the county. Less than 20% of the 200 school districts that used that program saw a decrease in graduation rates for students of color. Those schools that had a decrease in graduation rates could not delineate causation. However, this candidate was not going to change her opinion. So in the end, the best option for her was to change her topic, since her bias was overwhelming her research. She finally agreed, and her new topic was less confrontational and more constructive in helping her find solutions for her students.

CONSIDER YOUR INTENTIONS

What are your intentions? People often come into this part of the research journey by trying to prove or disprove something they have experienced in their profession or lives. The issue arises when the student is so intent on proving their point that they do not pursue all the perspectives beyond their own. In the end, you may accept the null hypothesis or find that your participants support the claims that previous research already illustrated. Either of these situations is an acceptable result. Accepting the null suggests that no statistical significance exists in a set of given observations (Creswell, 2009). Gaining data that supports what other studies have concluded does not mean the research was meaningless. That is far from the truth. Research that indicates that the null hypothesis is true or supports previous research helps extend our understanding of the topic. Instead of becoming discouraged, ask why the data may have led to the acceptance of the null hypothesis or why the qualitative analysis did not lead to new findings. The "why" could be a part of a recommendation for further research. The goal of the research is to learn—not always to prove you are right.

BEGIN WITH THE END IN MIND

In his book *The Seven Habits of Highly Effective People* (2004), Dr. Stephen Covey popularized the notion of beginning with the end in mind. The idea is simple: if you know where you are going, you can make the decisions necessary and take the right paths to get to the final destination. In the doctoral journey, the "end" is graduation, and often the journey culminates in the defense of a dissertation. So with this in mind, we are always considering how our decisions take us closer to the final goal of a terminal degree.

SAVING THE WORLD

Often, doctoral students are problem solvers and achievers! Many doctoral students dream of winning the Nobel Peace Prize for outstanding research in education. The desire for all the problems in the world to be solved by what we discover is both honorable and appealing. I wish we could all do that. At the least, you will be learning more about your topic, which may affect the way you do your job in the future. You may find out a factor that went undiscovered by your school district and may save millions of dollars. One of our students just conducted research that led his district to a potentially budget-saving conclusion. He discovered that the multi-million-dollar reading program which his school district had invested in really may not be as effective as advertised. It was an eye-opening discovery that his superintendent celebrated. However, this is a rare event. Most of you will not discover anything surprising, but you will learn something. What this process will teach you is how to research and evaluate issues that affect how organizations succeed. You can apply this process in the future and possibly discover something. In the end, we know there are big problems to solve, and you want to be part of the solution. This is an honorable mindset; however, when it comes to the dissertation, it is helpful to remember the story of the starfish:

> A young girl was walking along a beach upon which thousands of starfish had been washed up during a terrible storm. When she came to each starfish, she would pick it up, and throw it back into the ocean. People watched her with amusement.
> She had been doing this for some time when a man approached her and said, "Little girl, why are you doing this? Look at this beach! You can't save all these starfish. You can't begin to make a difference!"
> The girl seemed crushed, suddenly deflated. But after a few moments, she bent down, picked up another starfish, and hurled it as far as she could into the ocean. Then she looked up at the man and replied, "Well, I made a difference for that one!"
> The old man looked at the girl inquisitively and thought about what she had done and said. Inspired, he joined the little girl in throwing starfish back into the sea. Soon others joined, and all the starfish were saved.
> (adapted from Eiseley, 1968)

As you consider a topic for the dissertation and write each portion, know that this work is not meant to solve huge problems. Instead, explore a specific and distinct topic and consider how the data derived from your research may be helpful. Similar to the little girl and the starfish in the story, even if just one benefits from the findings of your research, you have contributed!

SUMMARY

Selecting a topic for research is difficult. Students tend to pick big topics and must narrow them down to a nuance of that topic. The struggle to let go of what they want to study down to what is possible to study in a limited timeline makes this progress frustrating at times, but stick with it. Students must let go of their personal agendas and explore all the avenues of that topic to find out the why and how of a phenomenon to expand the literature of the field of study. You will not always have an earth-shattering "Aha!" moment, but you will learn how to research to find solutions to future problems, and that is the purpose of the dissertation.

TRAVEL JOURNAL

- What topics are of interest to you?
- Why is this topic of interest?
- How might you avoid bias as you approach the topic for your dissertation?
- What steps can you take now to establish a clear destination and prepare your path for attaining a doctoral degree?
- What are you hoping to accomplish with your research?

PACKING CHECKLIST

- Select a topic and begin reading the current research.
- Narrow the topic into a specific issue that can be analyzed through qualitative or statistical analysis.
- Meet with a prospective chairperson and discuss your topic ideas. Create a plan for accomplishing your "end" goal of dissertation completion. This will assist you as you begin with the "end" in mind.

REFERENCES

Covey, S. R. (2004). *The 7 habits of highly effective people: Restoring the character ethic* (rev ed.). Free Press.

Creswell, J. W. (2009). *Research design: Qualitative, quantitative, and mixed methods approaches* (3rd ed.). Sage Publishing.

Eiseley, L. C. (1968). *"The Star Thrower" from the unexpected universe. Copywrite renewed in 1996 by Eichman III., J.A.* www.thestarfishchange.org/starfish-tale.

McGregor, S. (2018). *Understanding and evaluating research* (Vols. 1–0). SAGE Publications, Inc. https://doi.org/10.4135/9781071802656

Chapter 8

Your Tour Guides

CHAPTER OBJECTIVES

- Determine whether your program assigns or allows for electing a committee.
- Understand faculty and their roles.
- Evaluate committee options.
- Create a relationship with the committee.
- Learn from mistakes others have made.

INTRODUCTION

You are not alone on this journey. You do have tour guides in the guise of faculty members and university staff to help you along the way. Building healthy and professional relationships with those who are there to support you is a big key to success. If you are disrespectful or prideful during this process, the chances of you getting to the end of this journey with a diploma and a title could be delayed. All the faculty and staff that support doctoral programs are experienced in the process. The faculty have written dissertations themselves and clearly understand the challenges. Their purpose for being a part of this process is to help students and sometimes to do for them what wasn't done for themselves. This chapter will introduce you to the support staff that will guide you through this degree.

FACULTY IN THE PROGRAM

Becoming a faculty member in an education doctoral program is highly respected in academic circles. Becoming a faculty who has the professional and scholarly experience to work with candidates is not without its challenges. It is hard work. Most faculty members in the program not only teach more than one class but also may mentor numerous dissertation students through the research process. Most universities do not pay these faculty more money for this work. They may get a course release, but most commonly they get credit for university service, which will help them if they want to be promoted. Some faculty use candidate research to expand their own research agendas, thus increasing their number of publications. Please note that I am not referring to faculty as professors. Not all faculty members are professors. The title of *professor* is limited to a few members of a university faculty. There are fewer tenured professors. Most of the faculty at a university are assistant and associate professors, and many more adjuncts, instructors, lecturers, and various other faculty titles that are unique in some university communities. It might seem unimportant to you that there is a difference in faculty rankings, but in the academic world, titles are super important. Nothing makes a fully tenured professor angrier than someone calling an adjunct professor. I go more into the faculty ranks in the last chapter, because faculty rank is a culture like ranks in the military.

No matter what their official rank is, you will meet many of your faculty members in your classes, and this will give you an opportunity to get to know them well. This relationship-building opportunity will come in handy when you begin to create your dissertation or DiP committee. Some of the faculty from the university will not teach your classes but are also on the list for committee membership. As I have said many times in this book, your professional reputation is in full view in your classes, and the professors are watching, listening, and reading your work. As you know from your own experiences in school settings, teachers talk to each other and sometime commiserate when there are challenging students. They share both positive and negative experiences about students, so if you are not up to par, you may have slim pickings on your committee members. The committee faculty's names are on your dissertation, and no one wants to be associated with a poor research study.

YOUR CHAIRPERSON AND COMMITTEE

A dissertation/DiP chairperson is there to guide and support you through this research process. This faculty member wants you to be successful; however, he or she is not there to carry out your work. They will not always chase you down to find out about your progress. You need to contact them. You cannot take this relationship lightly. These faculty members usually have more than one student they are advising, so do not be surprised if they are busy. Keep them up to date on your progress and schedule face-to-face meetings at least once a semester to review your work. This relationship does not mean hanging out every day or sending them daily emails. Also, do not expect them to edit your papers or do your statistical analysis. If your chairperson is teaching one of your courses, you will have time to confer with them about your questions before or after class, if they allow that interaction. Some may prefer to have you talk to them during their office hours, so before- and after-class consultations are about the course topic and assignments. In the end, it is about knowing (or getting to know) your committee and their preferences. If you do not like your chairperson, work through it. Try not to burn bridges, because changing your chairperson can feel awkward and delay progress.

HOW TO PICK A CHAIRPERSON

When it comes to the dissertation, the chair is the tour guide. They will be leading you through some new research terrain, so it may be important to consider experience and personality type. Some prefer a disciplined approach of a dominant leader; others prefer a leader who will structure and support. It will be important to know yourself and recognize what type of leadership will assist you most through the dissertation process. If possible, choose a chair with this type of leadership style.

Many universities allow you to choose your chairperson. They should give you a list of faculty members who qualify for this position along with their curriculum vitae (CV). The CV, a document much like a résumé, but longer, will document all the research topics the faculty members have explored during their careers. You want to pick a person who has experience and some knowledge of your subject. This process should never be a popularity contest. Just because you like a faculty member does not mean they are appropriate to serve as your chairperson. You want someone who has a long record of supporting dissertation and research writing. This person should also have a reputation for being actively involved in the advising and writing process. Ask other doctoral students who are further in their program to give advice on this selection. You can also talk to the director of the program for support with this process. A bad dissertation chairperson can make your life miserable and delay the process and your graduation date.

If the institution does not allow a candidate to choose the committee chair, they will generally assign someone that they feel aligns with your research. Again, it will be important to establish a relationship, expectations, and a clear process for working toward your end goal of completion. Regardless of the way you derive your committee chair, embrace the opportunity to add a potential mentor to your network.

SNAPSHOT

It has been 11 years since I graduated with my doctoral degree. As I reflect, I am so thankful that I had the opportunity to gain the dissertation chair that I had. She was not my original choice, but when my chair retired, she stepped in to lead me through the process. To this day, she is still a mentor, and I highly respect her opinions. She has been a gift in navigating the higher education environment. My advice is to embrace the process, even when change or unexpected events occur.

HOW TO PICK COMMITTEE MEMBERS

You will also have the other professors from your university on your dissertation committee. One of the committee members is typically focused on the content of your study. You want someone who knows about your topic and can advise you on seeking sources and ideas. Another committee member may take on the role of methodologist. This person is one who can help you with the nuts and bolts of your research design. They should know qualitative methods or statistical design and help you with reliability and validity if you use a survey or questions. When you present your research at your preproposal/candidacy, proposal, and final defense, all committee members will be present to give you feedback. However, more importantly, these committee members should be present throughout the process of writing. Their feedback is valuable and will lead to a more polished dissertation.

Many students ask superintendents or supervisors in their school districts to act as outside members of the committee. This invitation can be good or bad. If your study is great, then you are promoting your expertise, which may lead to a promotion or job change. If your study is not good or poorly written, you may be putting your career in jeopardy. Be purposeful if this is a decision you pursue.

During the process of choosing the committee members, make sure to consult with your chair. Again, there are personalities to consider, and your chair may appreciate working with particular colleagues. Having a healthy team of committee members supporting you through the dissertation process will lead to a better research experience and dissertation completion. So invest time and energy up front to build relationships with those on your team.

WORST-CASE SCENARIOS DO HAPPEN

Life happens. Doctoral faculty leave the university either by choice (retire or move to another university) or they are asked to leave. It is very common to have the chairperson or committee memberschange. The department chair of the program will work with you to find a good option to fill any empty spots on your committee. It is useless energy to become upset or feel like this change is a roadblock. Universities are businesses, and personnel issues are the same in any organization. It is important for you not to get involved in university or department politics. Stay in your lane and focus on your research.

At the same time, doctoral students go through a lot of changes in their lives during their degree. Doctoral students get married, have babies (twins in one case), divorce, experience the death of a loved one, a promotion, or even a job loss. Almost everyone in doctoral programs is involved in demanding full-time jobs. As much as possible, plan for and prepare for these events. If something happens that may delay your writing progress or may affect your work or attendance in your course, do not be afraid to tell your chairperson and advisor. They are human and understand how life can disrupt even the best-laid plans. They cannot help you if you do not communicate to them about the challenges that face you. The goal is for you to finish your dissertation and graduate. However, if circumstances make it difficult to progress in the program, they are all willing to work with you to best accommodate your circumstances.

SNAPSHOT

One contributor explained that writing her dissertation was painful but her chair was helpful.

> Sitting down to focus—read and write—was really difficult because my mind was always elsewhere. I was constantly getting off task. At my yearly visit with my physician, he suggested testing me for ADD. Long story short . . . he put me on a low dose of ADD medication, and it worked wonders to get me through the process and helped me stay focused. It also helped me in all areas of life. I often wonder how my life would be different if I had been diagnosed earlier. I am not recommending or promoting ADD medication at all. I had not even thought about adults having ADD or ADHD, but I found out it is somewhat common. In the end, it helped me better understand what my students were going through when they were having a bad day due to ADD or ADHD. So many times, students with ADD or ADHD are just seen as bad children/students. Nothing is farther from the truth.

SNAPSHOT

Another contributor, Pete, noted the importance of a dissertation committee and timing.

> The dissertation committee chair is an integral part of the process of developing your hypothesis, planning the execution of the analysis, and writing and defending your dissertation.

About halfway through the doctoral program, far before ABD status, I learned that my committee chair was planning a sabbatical during the time my defense was projected to be scheduled. Considering how helpful, committed, and supportive she had been, this was not something favorable. The insecurity of knowing who might be covering for her and what changes might be required or occur approached trauma level.

I had some choices to make. I could continue my predicted schedule and accept the change in my committee and the other consequences. I could slow down, take fewer credits per term, or skip a term, if that was acceptable to the university. This option would have delayed my completion by about a full year. The final option was to accelerate my coursework and progress to be completed before the impending sabbatical.

Reviewing all the options, despite the incomplete course requirements and the plan for collecting and analyzing data, reporting it, and writing, editing, revising, revising, and defending the dissertation, I decided acceleration was the best choice. With the flexibility of a schoolteacher's summer, I was able to get approval for a course overload and registered for 21 credits for the May–July term. One of the courses was online only (years before COVID), and the reading and major assignment completed in three weeks, with weekly visits to the discussion board for review and comments. The other courses were manageable over the remainder of the summer term.

With those courses done, the remainder of the requirements were finished in time for my chair to supervise the completion and defense of the dissertation. The connection between the chair and the student continued, and the doctorate was awarded. Additionally, we co-authored a journal article on my topic.

So plan and consider your supporting team and all your options.

LESSONS IN HUMILITY

As stated before, most doctoral candidates are already working in the professional field of education or are leaders in businesses. It is important to remember that you are a doctoral candidate and your chair is the captain of the ship. Many candidates are leaders in their own organization and forget that in the doctoral environment, they are amateurs. Although you may be paying for your degree, that payment does not require faculty to be immediately available or bound by your demands. Faculty are teaching classes, advising students, writing their own research, and may have more than a few other doctoral candidates they are supporting. Please be patient and respectful of their positions and work.

When it comes to your dissertation, one way of showing respect is to provide a document free of errors. Many computer programs are available and designed to help with the editing of your document. Use them. Your dissertation chair is not an editor for your paper. In the end, if you feel that you need (or your chair states that you need) more than what editing software can provide, there are many great editors who can revise your document, and some institutions have these professionals available. So communicate with your dissertation chair and respect their preferences.

The following anecdotes come from faculty who have experienced some extreme situations and disrespect. Learn from their mistakes and, instead, create a healthy relationship with your faculty.

- *One student sent me her entire dissertation (all five chapters—over 100 pages) in the morning and asked me to have any feedback back to her by the end of that same day. She explained that her little girl was celebrating her fourth birthday and she would need to spend her upcoming spare time planning for that. If I could not give her feedback that day, she would not be able to turn in her final draft prior to the deadline (seven days away).*
- *Another candidate sent me a chapter to review around midnight on a Tuesday night. The next morning, Wednesday, at 7:00 a.m., he called concerned that he had not yet received feedback. When I questioned the time frames (maybe the email had been delayed or something had happened that caused me to mistake the timeline—surely, he was not expecting feedback in the middle of the night?), he verified that in fact he had sent it around midnight. He just thought maybe I had gotten the chance to review it—who needs sleep?*
- *I go to bed around 10:00 p.m. every night. When I woke up one morning, I found at least 10 missed calls, 20 text messages, and multiple emails from the same student. She was working on her paper from midnight to 3:00 a.m. Each message and email became more desperate and angrier in tone as the night went on. She wanted feedback and had questions about her research. She could not understand why I wouldn't "pick up the damn phone!"*

- A student turned in her paper with numerous spelling and grammar issues. You can see the number of words underlined in red and blue as MS Word generally does. Maybe she didn't understand what those lines meant. Instead of putting in the citations, she wrote, "CITE HERE." After reading a few pages, I quit reading and sent back some comments. I told her to only send me a paper that was "clean of any errors and had all citations correctly written." She emailed back in all caps and bold, **"THAT'S WHAT I PAY YOU TO DO!"** I withdrew from being the chair of her committee.
- A student was presenting his dissertation proposal, and I attended the presentation since his topic was similar to my own dissertation research. I sat next to one of his committee members, and the professor graciously allowed me to look at the manuscript. When I started reading, I realized that most of the paper was exactly like mine. The guy had lifted my paper and presented it as his own. I pulled up my paper to confirm the plagiarism and shared it with the committee member. He stopped the presentation and asked the student to leave the room. The committee was flabbergasted by the audacity of the student. When asked about plagiarism, he said, "Isn't this how it is done? I was allowed to do this on my master's thesis." He was dismissed from the program that day.

SUMMARY

Picking your support team that has experience in your area of study is essential for success. This selection is not a popularity contest but an educated decision on the right people for the research you are conducting. Your job is to work hard, communicate well, and treat the faculty and staff with respect. They all want you to succeed, but if you fight the process, you will be fighting alone, and that turns out well.

TRAVEL JOURNAL

- What styles of leadership do you most appreciate?
- What important traits will you look for in your dissertation chair?
- How will you create a relationship with your chair and committee?
- When you consider research and writing, what are your areas of strength and weakness?
- Who would you like to join your committee?

PACKING CHECKLIST

- Brainstorm some potential committee members and chairs. Consider leadership styles, personalities, and content knowledge.
- Meet your chairperson (if possible); get their email address and phone number. Ask them how they handle communication with their students and what are their expectations of you and your study.
- Work with your chairperson on the method of your study and the data you will need. Discuss the reliability and validity of any instrument you plan to use.

Chapter 9

The Voyage

CHAPTER OBJECTIVES

- Align elements of your dissertation.
- Evaluate the components associated with Chapters 1–5 of the dissertation.
- Analyze your schedule and pace yourself.

INTRODUCTION

The biggest and most crucial challenge of achieving any doctoral degree is the doctoral dissertation. This research project may be the most extensive paper you have ever written in your life. The aim is to test a hypothesis, evaluate a program, or answer questions related to leadership in organizations. The impact of your research may influence public policy or reveal a new perspective on an issue affecting schools or organizations. During this chapter, we will discover what the voyage of the dissertation is like. Chapters 1–5 of the dissertation will be discussed, as well as tools for the journey.

ALIGNMENT IN RESEARCH

Once you have your topic in mind (see Chapter 7 for insights on this process) and have read significant research, it is time to create your study. The most critical components of your dissertation include the title, problem, purpose, research questions, framework, design, data collection instrument, and analysis. These eight elements must be aligned. If the vertebrae in your back get out of alignment, you may feel some pain. The same is true of the dissertation. If the elements of your dissertation differ and there is no logical connection between these areas, you may question your direction or compromise your research clarity. Before you dig into the details of Chapters 1–5, take a moment to consider the eight elements noted earlier. Document the clear connection between each component, and ask colleagues or your dissertation chair to provide feedback to you.

ABSTRACT

You do not write the abstract until after you have written Chapters 1–3 and are preparing for your proposal defense. This section may be limited by a word count and is a description of your study. Your abstract tells readers what they will find in your dissertation. **Context + problem + main point** (Booth et al., 2008). Booth et al. (2008) also suggest that students begin with a couple of sentences establishing the background of the study based on other research, continue with a statement of the problem, and conclude with the main result of the study. *You write in the future tense* until you complete your study (Chapters 4 and 5). Then, you will go back, rewrite the abstract in the past tense, and reflect on the findings of your study.

CHAPTER 1: INTRODUCTION

This chapter is where you write a narrative hook, which means you write to engage your readers or "hook" the reader into the study. The first section is a brief review of the issues surrounding your topic. After this brief introduction (three to five pages), you will describe the study. You will *write in the future tense* since you have not completed your study yet. When you are writing Chapters 4 and 5, you will go back and change the verb tense to past tense.

Chapter 1 includes the following subtopics:

- **Introduction.** Summary of literature about your research topic (you can reuse this literature in your Chapters 2 and 5).
- **Statement of the problem.** What problems or issues lead to a need for the study?
- **Theoretical framework.** Select a theory that closely aligns with the topic. It is the lens through which one can view how the research problem exists. Do not pick more than two theories to support your framework. More than two can confuse your readers and bog you down. Kerlinger and Lee (2000) define and explain the meaning of a theory very well, as follows:

A theory is a set of interrelated constructs (concepts), definitions, and propositions that present a systematic view of phenomena by specifying relations among variables, to explain and predict the phenomena. This definition says three things: (1) a theory is a set of propositions consisting of defined and interrelated constructs, (2) a theory sets out the interrelations among a set of variables (constructs), and in so doing, presents a systematic view of the phenomena described by the variables, and (3) a theory explains phenomena; it does so by specifying which variables are related to which variables and how they are related, thus enabling the researcher to predict from certain variables to certain other variables.

(p. 11)

> **SNAPSHOT** 📷
>
> At first, the concept of a theoretical framework threw my cohort for a loop. In our second semester, we were asked to build a theoretical framework for our dissertations in progress (which we'd only just begun). We went into it without a clear understanding of a theoretical framework's purpose or how it connected to our coursework. None of us have kept the framework that we created in that assignment for our current dissertation in practice (DiP). I think we all wish that we'd had a better introduction to the dissertation as a whole and the theoretical framework that guides it. We figured it out eventually, but I know that many of us were frustrated by the time that was lost by having to re-read, re-research, and refine our theoretical frameworks. Some of that would have naturally occurred as we refined our studies, but if we'd had a clearer understanding from the start, we would have been spared some grief!
>
> —Katherine Ramp, EdD

- **Purpose of the study.** Sets the objectives, the intent, and the central idea for the study. This is where you establish the rationale for your study, and the purpose should be closely aligned with your problem statement.
- **Research questions.** These are questions that are guiding the design of your study. They are broader than the ones that you might ask in an interview but are intended to frame your study. If you are conducting interviews, focus groups, or surveys, you should use these questions to guide you as you create the interview protocols or survey instruments. If you are using a quantitative instrument with established validity, the research questions must align with the variables being measured by the instrument(s). As you create these, consider the problem and the purpose and make sure to connect these to create alignment. A section on hypotheses should also be included if this is a quantitative design.

- **Definition of terms.** The glossary of terms you use may be educational jargon so people out of the profession can understand your study (Creswell, 2009). There is often a need to operationalize terms to give the reader a clearer understanding, and this is the location to do this. If there are multiple meanings in society for specific verbiage you plan to use, include and define these for clarity. Each definition should be written in your own words (no direct quotes) but should include a citation.
- **Limitations.** Every study, no matter how well conducted, has some limitations. It is not reasonable to use the words "prove" and "disprove" concerning research findings. It is always possible that future research will cast doubt on the validity of any hypothesis or the conclusions from a study. Write what you anticipate as the limitations of your study. Also, note how you plan to minimize potential limitations of your research design. If the environment or situation changes as you conduct research, you may edit this upon the completion of your study.

As you write Chapter 1, consider some elements from Chapter 3. Creswell (2009) suggests one to two central research questions for qualitative research, at least three questions for a mixed-method study, and for quantitative research, employing 0 to 4 research questions may be appropriate. Now you must determine what data you need to answer your questions.

One of the most challenging stages when writing your first chapter is the process of deciding what to say. "Writer's block" is a common condition at this point. First, you probably have not written anything like this, and you may not know how exactly to start. You also might feel like you should write scholarly (even if you do not feel it) to fit the degree you are seeking. Relax. The best way to start is to write your thoughts about the topic. You may even choose to start writing Chapter 2 rather than beginning with Chapter 1. This is a great option, since understanding the research and creating the literature review are paramount to the dissertation process. Try not to place too much pressure on yourself at this point; there is no expectation of perfection in your ability to express yourself in a scholarly way at this point.

It is important to emphasize that *this paper is not about you*. The dissertation is about an important topic and its influence on leadership and reform. While you have much experience as a leader, this experience is not a part of the writing and researching process. Do not refer to yourself in the first person or even as "the researcher." Including your experiences or your opinions too soon will weaken your argument and your study. You do not want to give the readers an idea that you are biased in your data collection or results. You will get the opportunity in the last chapter to reflect on your opinions based on your findings on this topic.

CHAPTER 2: LITERATURE REVIEW

This chapter is the most extensive section of your paper and can exceed 50 pages in length. In this chapter, you describe all the nuances of your topic based on the previously conducted research. Read as much as you can on your topic and then create an outline of the most common subtopics. Then, look for patterns in other literature to assist your writing. You are telling the story based on past studies about your topic. While there is no limitation to the number of studies or the dates of the studies you will use, make sure you focus on as many current studies as possible. Most institutions require citations from within the past five years to support the need for your study and provide readers with a solid foundation of recent relevant information. Focusing your efforts on current literature will also help you in your analysis of the current gaps that exist in research which your study can help fill.

As you read, you will identify the researchers who are the leaders in the field you are studying. Use their bibliographies or references to glean more facets about your topic. You will be amazed at what you might find. Consider yourself a detective searching for all the clues associated with your topic. Organize similar trends in folders or binders or within reference management software. Color-coding with highlighters or using online tools to help with this process can be helpful when you need to support your findings in Chapter 4.

There are two sides to every issue. Address the antithesis of your study as a significant discussion thread. No study is substantial if it is one-sided. You will want to create a complete picture of your topic's components, even if you disagree with them.

One common mistake that thesis writers make at this stage is to make this section a continuous series of quotations. However, this is not the intended purpose of Chapter 2. Write transitions between thoughts to build the background of the study. Read other literature reviews to see how the writers develop their arguments.

It is critical to remember the purpose of Chapter 2 is to compare and contrast what has been researched in the area that you are investigating. Comparing and contrasting is impossible without multiple viewpoints, so virtually every paragraph in Chapter 2 should have two or more authors and citations. One of the most frequent mistakes in the literature review occurs when the writer summarizes one research study and then moves forward and summarizes the next study. This is the process for creating an annotated bibliography but differs from the literature review. Instead of jumping from article to article as you would for an annotated bibliography, synthesize, compare, and connect the different research articles for the reader.

Another mistake the thesis writer may make in this section is to forget to cite their resources. It is easy to be engrossed in writing, look back, and forget where you found the quotation or idea. Set up your references and cite correctly from the beginning. It will save you time, worry, and aggravation in the end.

Finding Research for Literature Reviews

There are many ways to research your topic. Google Scholar is a great search engine. Go to your university library website, and you can search ERIC for articles and download books. The days of searching microfiche and photocopying articles in the library are long gone. (For those of you under the age of 50, you may not understand this revelation.) For every article you find, look at their references to search for more articles. You can also ask your professors for ideas for further research.

Create a reference page, and copy the citation of the article or book right away. You may or may not use this article or book, but you do not want to lose the citation in the end if you do. If you use ERIC, they have a place where you can copy the APA citation and paste it into your references. (Note: you will have to check the citation for the correct format since APA changes the format from time to time.) Microsoft Word 10 has a feature for managing references and citations. Look under the "References" tab for "managing" your sources, citations, and reference section. In addition, there are many online reference tools to help with this process. If you choose to use an online tool, always double-check the reference and link to verify that it is APA-compliant.

References vs. Bibliography

Many students use the terms *references* and *bibliography* interchangeably. The two lists of resources you use in your research are different. A *bibliography* is all the literature you find on your topic. The list can be endless. Every time you find an article or research on your topic, add it to your bibliography with the correct APA citation. If you are using your university library, they have a link on the site of the article that gives you the correct APA citation, so copy and paste in alphabetical order on your bibliography. Microsoft has a section under "References" where you can store your bibliography and set the style, that is, APA. One professor gives a 100-day/100-article challenge for his dissertation students. He asks them to read one article every day for 100 days about their topic. They turn in the bibliography to him, and they win a T-shirt. This forces his students to read a variety of articles and various points of view about their topic before writing one word.

Once you have collected all the articles you can find, then create a reference page. The articles on the reference page are only for the articles you cite in your paper. Do not include any articles you don't use in your actual paper. Simply stated, the *bibliography* is all articles, and the *reference* is only what you use. Check with your university program's policy on the expectations of a bibliography and reference pages for your research.

Organizing Your Research Articles

Personal organization is a matter of style. How do you want to save the articles you are using in your research? Some people download articles onto their computers. If you do this, create folders surrounding each subtopic of your study. It will make it easier to find what you need when you get to that topic. Make sure you back up your folders on a flash drive or in the cloud!

Other people must have hard copies so they can highlight important points. If you go this route, buy lots of paper, toner, and binders. You can organize your hard copies in a few ways. One way is to group articles per binder and put a cover page in the front of the binder with the authors and titles of the articles. Color-code with tabs or highlighters you can find at any office supply store. If you assign one color per subtopic, it makes it easier to find the information you need while writing. Another way to organize your articles is to put common themes in individual folders. Each folder should have some way for you to access information by either tabs or color codes.

Others may choose an online program that helps with organizing. Various programs offer the ability to segment a project into bite-size pieces and store articles. Your institution may offer a subscription to a program of this nature, or you may choose to utilize a free or paid service. Regardless of the method you choose for organization, the important part is that you make every effort to organize materials early in the dissertation process. The time invested will pay off in the end.

CHAPTER 3: METHODOLOGY

Qualitative, Quantitative, or Mixed Methods?

Research design is an essential question concerning your study. You will likely take several research and statistics courses to help you make this decision. In basic terms, *qualitative research* is exploring and understanding the meaning individuals or groups ascribe to a social or human problem (Creswell, 2009, p. 232). You can do this through interviews, case studies, and questionnaires. *Quantitative research* means testing objective theories by exploring the relationship between variables. Statistical procedures can measure these variables. *Mixed method* is a combination of both qualitative and quantitative forms of research.

If you are a person where the thought of statistics gives you the sweats, do not allow that fear to keep you from conducting a significant quantitative study. There are faculty and staff at your university that will help you. Your methodologist and your chairperson are also there to walk you through this process.

This chapter serves as the backbone of your thesis. You will write the what, who, why, and how of your research study. **You write this** chapter in the future tense because it comes before you conduct your study. Chapter 3 includes the following subheadings:

- **Research design.** What is the type of study you are planning to do? Qualitative, quantitative, or mixed-method? Why? The design of your study must align and be suitable for your research question(s). Generally, research questions that begin with "how" or "why" are answered through qualitative designs. Regardless of the design you choose, make sure to cite experts recognized for experience with that specific design.
- **Research questions.** These are the questions that will frame and guide your study. Use the same verbiage as you did in Chapter 1. Each time these are mentioned, it is critical that they remain written the same.
- **Setting.** From where are you getting your data? If it is a school district or organization, describe it as much as possible. Demographic information is acquired from federal, state, local, or corporate websites.
- **Subjects/participants.** What type of population do you include in your study? Teachers? Students? Principals? Superintendents? Parents? Describe what you know so far. Give a clear understanding of exactly who will be included in your study. This information is critical as the IRB assesses your research. Their primary purpose is to protect participants, so knowing exactly who will be included in your study helps them analyze potential vulnerabilities.
- **Procedures.** This is a detailed description of the process you will conduct during your study. You will begin by getting permission from the school district or agency to gather the data. You must document every step in this section. Think of it as if you were writing the directions for a recipe. Do not assume everyone will naturally know each step of your research process, even if it feels trivial.
- **Instruments.** What instruments are you using to gather your data? Interview protocols? A survey? If you are creating interview questions or a survey, use your research questions to guide the creation of the instrument. The instrumentation must align with the research questions and design of the study. The chairperson should assist you through this process.
- **Data collection.** Include a step-by-step process that you plan to take to collect data. For each instrument, describe the technology or software which will be utilized, frequency, duration, and method for recording all data. Also, explain how participants will exit the collection process. Will there be any follow-up or debriefing?
- **Data analysis.** Describe procedures for the organization of data. Identify software and procedures for cleaning and understanding data. Select an evidence-based model or statistical test which is appropriate based on the design of your study.

- **Reliability/validity.** Describe the methods and strategies that you will employ to increase reliability and validity in your study, or discuss the instrument validity if a quantitative approach is utilized.
- **Ethical procedures.** Explain the procedures you will maintain to ensure participant protection. Refer to appendices to illustrate compliance with institutional requirements.

Do some of these subtitles look familiar? You wrote some of this in Chapter 1, and you are repeating this in Chapter 3. You can copy/paste some of what you wrote in Chapter 1 (the problem, purpose, and research questions should always be stated the same), but make sure to vary other portions of your writing. Varying sentence structure can create a more inviting environment for the reader, though there are a few times in your paper you will be repeating the same thing.

Collecting Data

Many students rely on archival data or secondary data that is already available through agencies or districts. This data would have been collected for a previous purpose, so often focusing on this type of data will expedite the IRB approval process (which will be discussed later). If you choose to use this type of data, you must get permission from the agency or district before using the data. Contact the research departments of the agency or district for the policy or instructions for using their data. Even if you have access to the data through your job, you must ask permission to use the data. Some districts will allow you to use the data for a study; however, they will have specific guidelines they want you to follow to protect the employees or students in their district. It is common for a district to restrict their name, school name, or student name. In that case, you can describe the district as "a large, urban school district located near the Gulf Coast of Texas," for example. Some districts have a policy that requires a researcher to send a copy of the final paper to them when they are finished. Other districts or agencies require a fee for accessing their data. In the end, approval of the research is at the discretion of the organization, so establishing communication with someone early is strongly encouraged.

If you choose to create a survey or interview questions, piloting the instrument and conducting a field study are often recommended to enhance content validity (Creswell, 2009). Before this, IRB permission must be obtained as well as site permission (permission from the school district, organization, or group to recruit participants). Any participants active in interviews, focus groups, or surveys must sign a consent form. Check with your university or chair for a consent form example. For online surveys, you can add consent information at the beginning of the survey. *Often, the institution or **IRB** requires consent forms and responses from the interviews, surveys, and data to be kept at* *the university or in your possession for three to seven years after your study is complete. Again, make sure to know the policies of your university before beginning research.*

As you complete the proposal (first three chapters of the dissertation), make sure to include a copy of the letter (site approval) from the district, organization, or group in the appendix of your doctoral thesis. The proposal is typically used to create your IRB application. You will need to scan the district/agency permission letters and upload them on your IRB. Even if you plan to use archival or secondary data (open and available from previous years), you must attain approval from the organization for data based on human subjects. The form will be provided to you by your chairperson.

Institutional Review Boards (IRBs) and Protection of Human Subjects

Every institution that supports research must have an institutional review board (IRB) that reviews all proposed research. You will take a training course like CITI training before you submit your proposal to the board. They will ask for specific information about your study, questions, subjects, explanation of your statistical design, and limitations. Copy/paste all this information from your paper to the IRB application. Do not deviate from your paper. The purpose of the proposal defense is to make sure you have everything written correctly before you submit it for human subjects research.

The IRB committee is composed of faculty from all over your university. This is another reason you should explain all professional jargon and acronyms. If the faculty member is a professor in fine arts or liberal arts, they may not understand your profession's worldview; however, they are very skilled in the knowledge of appropriate research methods. Most university IRB committees meet monthly. A calendar is typically posted online with the application deadlines and the committee meeting dates. This process may take a few months if you miss deadlines. If you submit your application on the last day of the deadline, there is little chance for you to be on the agenda for the upcoming meeting. Please do not push for an exception.

The IRB process is designed to protect participants, so they will err on the side of caution. Very few students are approved during the first submission to most institutions. The IRB committee will send corrections for you to make. Do not allow this to discourage you. Answer their questions in a Word document, and make the corrections on your application. Review the application with your chairperson, and after their approval, resubmit your application. The biggest issue arises when students wait too long to fill out these applications. After your proposal is defended, you want to complete this process; then, you can start your study and graduate in a timely fashion. Talk to your chairperson if you have difficulty with this process.

You should use your completed Chapter 3 to request site approval. You can copy/paste from your paper to make this process easier, consistent, and coherent. The committee members or personnel at the site where you seek permission to conduct the study are not always knowledgeable of educational jargon or public school processes, so you must describe everything in detail. Do not assume they will understand what you are explaining in your study. You will repeat your procedures often. Do not write any abbreviations. You will upload a copy of the instruments, interview protocol, questionnaires, observations, and consent forms, which your participants must sign before moving forward with the study. Include the consent form, site approval letter, and any instrument in the appendix of your proposal and dissertation.

STOP HERE: Do not interview, survey, or request any data before IRB and organizational approval.

District, Agency, and Human Subjects Applications for Research

You will use this chapter when completing your human subjects application for the institutional review board (IRB) required for all research studies at your university. There will be more information about human subjects applications later in this book. It is important to stress that you should write Chapter 3 before writing applications for research for agencies, districts, or human subjects. You must be consistent with what data you want to use in all applications or site approvals. Check with your chairperson to review your thought process about your study. **NOTE: Your whole committee must approve your study after successfully passing the proposal defense before filling out any applications or IRB documentation.**

CHAPTER 4: RESULTS

After you conduct your study and analyze data, you write Chapter 4 and discuss your findings and results. You will explain your results, whether they are in the form of themes or statistical information. *At this point, write in the past tense and revise the rest of the dissertation accordingly.* Include charts and graphs of your data to help you communicate your results. The purpose of Chapter 4 is to answer the research questions, so make sure this receives focus as you write Chapter 4.

Do not panic if you are not well-versed in statistical or qualitative analysis. You will take courses related to research, and your chairperson or methodologist will guide you during this process.

In the case that any deviations to the research plan in Chapter 3 occurred, these should be noted at the beginning of Chapter 4. For instance, if you had planned to utilize Zoom but instead utilized Microsoft Teams, this would be considered a minor deviation from your research plan and could be noted at the beginning of Chapter 4. Always consult your dissertation chair prior to making changes to your study. No matter how small they may seem, deviations may cause one to need additional IRB approvals.

Chapter 4 typically includes the following subheadings:

- **Introduction.**
- **Data analysis/results.** This is your chance to speak about the results of your study and answer your research questions based on your data.
- **Reliability/validity.** In this section, discuss how validity and reliability were maintained. How did you implement those processes that were described in Chapter 3?
- **Conclusion.**

Make statements of the results without any implication, speculation, assessment, evaluation, or interpretation. In general, keep the results and the conclusions and discussion separate. Your data analysis (presentation, interpretation, explanation) must be consistent with the research questions or hypotheses and the study's underlying theoretical framework.

- Check the consistency of hypothesis/research questions between Chapters 1, 3, and 4.
- Check: Are the analyses consistent with Chapter 3?

In the concluding section of Chapter 4, outcomes should be logically and systematically summarized and interpreted concerning their importance to the research questions and hypotheses.

CHAPTER 5: CONCLUSIONS AND DISCUSSION OF THE RESULTS

Chapter 5 is a narrative of results and discusses the implications of your study in the world of education. The goal of this chapter is to give meaning to the results that you reported in Chapter 4.

Chapter 5 includes the following subheadings:

- **Introduction.** The chapter begins with a brief overview of the why and how of the study. It reviews the questions or issues addressed and a summary of the findings.
- **Discussion of results (interpretations).**
  - Includes conclusions that address all the research questions.
  - Contains references to outcomes in Chapter 4.

- Covers all the data.
- Is bounded by the evidence collected.
- Relates the findings to a larger body of literature on the topic, including the conceptual/theoretical framework.

- **Recommendations.** Provides advice for practical research-based changes in policies or practices.
- **Implications for leaders.** Make sure the implications are grounded in the significance section of Chapter 1 and outcomes presented in Chapter 4. Express the implications in terms of tangible improvements to individuals, communities, organizations, and institutions. Identify and describe methodological, theoretical, and/or empirical implications for stakeholders and leadership.
- **Implications for further research.**

Action

- It should flow logically from the conclusions and contain steps to helpful action.
- Describe the type of professionals who need to pay attention to the results of your study.
- Indicate how the results might be disseminated.

Further Study

- Point to topics that need closer examination and may generate a new round of questions.

- **Conclusion.** This includes a reflection on the researcher's experience with the research process. The researcher discusses possible personal biases, the possible effects on the participants or the situation, and changes in thinking because of the study. The work closes with a strong concluding statement, making the "take-home message" clear to the reader.

Writing Suggestions for Chapter 5

- *Address counterarguments.*
  - Pretending there are not two sides does not make one side accurate.
  - "After the interviews of the teachers at Alpha School, it was discovered that all teachers hate the No Child Left Behind Act."
  - Tackle the best points of the other side.
  - Look for intersections.
  - This process is not a cage match; it is research.

- *Avoid generalizations.*

  Generalizations encourage blanket or sweeping statements.
  Example: "All," "every," "none," "never."

- *Avoid logical fallacies.*

  - Slippery slope fallacy:

    If we commit to action A, it will invariably lead to dramatic and negative outcome Z (A > Z).

    "If we do not work with at-risk middle school boys in reading, they will inevitably end up in jail."

  - Correlation vs. causation confusion:

    "After the remedy, test scores improved."
    The rooster crowing before dawn does not mean that his noise made the sunrise.

- **Be humble.**

  Avoid praising yourself too much.
  Example: "The methods outlined in Chapter 3 represent a breakthrough in the design of distributed systems . . ."

  - *Avoid Criticizing Yourself Too Much*

  Example: "Although the technique employed in the current study was not earthshaking . . ."

Dissertation Sections

This list is an example of the potential dissertation sections (note: this list is not exhaustive; check your university's requirements for section headings):

1. Blank page
2. Copyright page
3. Title page with month and year of your graduation
4. Signature page with the month and year of your graduation
5. Acknowledgments
6. Abstract title page
7. Abstract
8. Table of contents
9. List of tables
10. List of figures (illustrations)
11. Body of paper (Chapters 1–5)

12. References
13. Appendices
14. Approved IRB and site approval
15. Vita (optional)

REMEMBER TO BREATHE, BUT ALSO KEEP WRITING!

People panic at the immensity of this project. This paper can scare even the bravest and most experienced writers. You are now wondering if you can handle all this work, just like a beginning marathon runner looking at that 26.2-mile run and wondering if it is humanly possible to run that far without having a heart attack. Calm your fears; this is possible, and you can manage this ordeal while keeping your job, relationships, health, and sanity.

Make continuous progress and keep writing. Many candidates find it beneficial to set aside specific times and write. Even just 30 minutes per day can get paragraphs written and the dissertation is done. Stay consistent and remember to be thorough. This paper must be over 100 pages long. "If the thesis is under 100 pages, it better make me cry," said Dr. Angus MacNeil, Professor, University of Houston. In total, your thesis contains five chapters. Many professors refer to chapters when discussing your thesis, so it is crucial to understand each chapter.

PACE YOUR PROGRESS

Athletes know that to train appropriately, they need to develop a good training routine. It is dangerous to develop a pace too quickly. The most successful athletes have trainers who develop a training schedule in progress so the athlete does not injure himself. No runner starts his training running 18 miles but starts in four- to five-mile runs.

This metaphor might sound silly, but writing your doctoral thesis is very similar in concept. Right now, you are thinking, "How in the world will I write all this and not start smoking and drinking to relieve the stress?" The stress you will have, but your university program can help minimize this stress by breaking down the process into smaller bite pieces. Again, watch your time management, or you will risk burnout.

SUMMARY

Though the dissertation may be the longest paper that you have ever written, it can be broken down into chapters and accomplished by focusing on one element at a time. Keeping alignment in mind, one can test a hypothesis, evaluate a program, or answer questions related to leadership in organizations. Continuous incremental writing and pacing yourself are two strategies that you may find beneficial during the process.

REFLECTING ON YOUR JOURNEY

- As you consider the chapters of the dissertation, is there one chapter that seems like it may be most challenging?
- What elements of the dissertation seem most intuitive to you?
- How will you manage your time so you can concentrate on writing the dissertation?

PACKING CHECKLIST

- Write an outline of your literature review. This outline will also help you create other chapters and focus on alignment.
- Come up with a system for organizing your research articles.
- Create your reference page.
- Review your schedule with supervisors and family so they know what your plan is for organizing your time.

REFERENCES

Booth, W. C., Colomb, G. G., & Williams, J. W. (2008) *The craft of research*. The University of Chicago Press.

Creswell, J. W. (2009). *Research design: Qualitative, quantitative, and mixed methods approaches* (3rd ed.). Sage Publishing.

Kerlinger, F. N., & Lee, H. B. (2000). *Foundations of behavioural research* (4th ed.). Cengage Learning.

Chapter 10

Documenting Your Journey

CHAPTER OBJECTIVES

- Evaluate your presentation skills.
- Determine requirements for presentations for your program.
- Analyze presentation requirements during your doctoral program.

INTRODUCTION

Throughout your time as a doctoral candidate, you may give several presentations to your committee where you will discuss your research study. These presentations are an opportunity to share your progress with your committee and to gain feedback. A journey could never be complete without documenting the details of the trip; likewise, the presentations give you an opportunity to document progress. The committee will give you specific suggestions and may challenge you on your topic and research goals. Consider this a time to enhance your research plans and create the most scholarly research study possible. In the beginning, if you have the opportunity to present a preproposal or proposal, do not be surprised if the committee suggests a different direction for your research. Trust them. Implement the feedback and revisions your committee requests in a timely fashion and then move forward with the research process. This chapter will provide some basics to remember when presenting research, concepts associated with some of the most critical presentations associated with the doctoral process, and ideas for slide topics that may be included during each benchmark presentation.

PRESENTATION BASICS

Some presentation basics may benefit you as you prepare presentations for your research. First, it is important to remember the 5×5 principle (Wellstead et al., 2017). The idea is that you should only have five lines of text and five words across. This creates a simple slide design free from verbose thought. Wellstead et al. (2017) also note that a light-colored background with dark text is easier to read than a dark background. Blome et al. (2017) recommend the following practices when presenting research:

- Keep the slides simple.
- Know the audience.
- Make eye contact.
- Rehearse and familiarize yourself with the presentation.
- Do not read from the slides.
- Limit the number of lines and words per slide.
- Be aware of time limits.

Keeping these ideas in mind may assist you in preparing for your preproposal, proposal, oral defense, or other presentation expectation. Maintaining professional poise and dressing appropriately will also assist you as you move forward.

PREPROPOSAL/CANDIDACY DEFENSE

The preproposal presentation may take place during the beginning portion of your dissertation journey. Not all universities require preproposals, so check with your institution on the exact requirements for your degree. The preproposal is designed to ensure you are on the right track before you go too far along with your research. You will create a PowerPoint presentation discussing your research. It would be best to have a title page, signature pages, Chapters 1–2, a portion of Chapter 3, and references completed. This presentation is not a "death by PowerPoint" situation. Be brief, illustrate clear alignment, and summarize your plan. Committee members are looking at your study with a critical eye to verify the viability of the research. Bring copies of your paper or presentation for each committee member. Do not be surprised if the committee asks you to make significant changes to your study. They want you to conduct a meaningful study, and they are aware of the limitations you might face—trust them.

Slide titles may include: title page, statement of the problem, purpose, research questions, literature review (subtopics with principal studies and researchers), setting, participants, instruments, data collection procedures, analysis (if you know), and limitations of the study.

DEADLINES AND TIME FRAMES

Programs typically have deadlines for the completion of your dissertation and time frames required for committee review. Check with your chairperson for the protocol at the university you choose. The key is that each committee member should have a chance to read your paper before you present it. The document should be publication-ready and in the correct format before sending it for committee review. Pages such as the dedication or acknowledgments may not be necessary until your final defense.

PROPOSAL DEFENSE

This presentation takes place after your preproposal/candidacy defense and generally occurs after comprehensive exams. You should have Chapters 1–3 completed along with an abstract. You will create a PowerPoint to summarize Chapters 1–3. Again, be brief and be prepared to explain all the aspects of your study. This presentation should not last more than 30 minutes, but do ask your chairperson for their expectations of this presentation.

Often, the proposal will be announced, and guests can attend. Bring copies of your PowerPoint and paper for each committee member. Dress professionally and be on time. The proposal defense is generally completed just before submission to your institutional IRB. Revisions and feedback may need to be applied after the proposal. Once the committee approves your proposal, the IRB process is typically the next step; after IRB approval is gained, you can begin the study. So prepare as much as possible with the help of your dissertation chair.

Slide titles may include: title page, statement of the problem, purpose, research questions, literature review (subtopics with principal studies and researchers), setting, subjects, instruments, analysis, data collection procedures, and limitations of the study. This presentation should be more detailed than the preproposal/candidacy defense.

DISSERTATION DEFENSE

The dissertation defense is the culminating presentation of the doctoral program. As you complete your research, writing, and editing of the dissertation, consider the dissertation defense the showcase for all your hard work. In advance of the defense, work closely with your chair and committee to organize materials in the method they recommend. Traditionally, the dissertation defense focuses on the data, findings, and recommendations of your research. This benchmark should only be completed upon finalization of the dissertation paper. For this reason, it is important to verify that the committee has sufficient time to review the document. As stated earlier in the chapter, most institutions set guidelines or deadlines for the timing of dissertation defenses, so make sure to check with your dissertation chair.

Slide titles may include: title page, statement of the problem, research questions, literature review (subtopics with principal studies and researchers), setting, subjects, instruments, limitations of the study, data collection procedures, analysis, findings, conclusions, and recommendations.

SUMMARY

Dissertation presentations are an opportunity to share your progress with your committee and to gain feedback. The committee will give you specific suggestions and may challenge you on your topic and research goals. Maintain communication with the committee throughout the process to ensure you meet their expectations during each presentation that your institution requires. Implement the feedback and revisions your committee requests in a timely fashion and then move forward with the research process. This chapter has provided some basics to remember when presenting research, concepts associated with some of the most critical presentations associated with the doctoral process, and ideas for slide topics that may be included during each benchmark presentation.

TRAVEL JOURNAL

- What strengths and weaknesses do you have when presenting?
- How will you work on presentation skills throughout your entire doctoral program?
- Who would you like to invite to your presentations?

PACKING CHECKLIST

- Meet with your chairperson at the beginning of each semester to discuss dates for your presentations. If changes occur which will delay or prevent a presentation, discuss these.
- Create an outline of presentation topics. Remember to be clear, concise, and aligned in your research.

REFERENCES

Blome, C., Sondermann, H., & Augustin, M. (2017). Accepted standards on how to give a medical research presentation: A systematic review of expert opinion papers. *GMS Journal for Medical Education, 34*, 1–7. www.ncbi.nlm.nih.gov/pmc/articles/PMC5327661/

Wellstead, G., Whitehurst, K., Gundogan, B., & Agha, R. (2017). How to deliver an oral presentation. *International Journal of Surgery: Oncology, 2*(6), e25. https://doi.org/10.1097/IJ9.0000000000000025

Chapter 11

The Final Defense

CHAPTER OBJECTIVES

- Understand the process of the dissertation defense.
- Evaluate the components associated with the dissertation defense.
- Examine the typical process of the dissertation defense.

INTRODUCTION

The dissertation defense is the culminating presentation of the doctoral program. As you complete your research, writing, and editing of the dissertation, consider the dissertation defense the showcase for all your hard work. In advance of the defense, work closely with your chair and committee to organize materials in the method they recommend. Traditionally, the dissertation defense focuses on the data, findings, and recommendations of your research. This benchmark should only be completed upon completion of all five chapters of the dissertation. For this reason, it is important to verify that the committee has sufficient time to review the document. This chapter will provide important information about the final dissertation defense, a checklist for preparation, and some future steps.

FINAL DEFENSE

This presentation is the pinnacle of your program. In short, this is the time when you will explain the whole study. This special event will end with a celebration with your family and colleagues. Do not be surprised if the committee asks for revisions. They will not sign off unless they feel confident that your research is sound and accurate. Those who are on the committee will be named in the dissertation, so the credibility of the research is of utmost importance to the entire team.

You are getting ready to present your final defense. These are a few tips to help you prepare for the big day. *You must get your chairperson's and committee's*

THE FINAL DEFENSE

approval before planning the defense date. The university will typically announce your defense so that guests may attend. Other doctoral students may choose to attend in preparation of their dissertation defense. Do not let this worry you. They cannot be in the room while the professors deliberate.

FINAL DEFENSE CHECKLIST

1. You must send your paper (Chapters 1–5, including the abstract) to your committee members ten days (or sometimes more, depending on the institution) before the defense.
   a. Make sure pages are numbered correctly and the spacing is correct.
   b. Check APA and institutional guidelines for the dissertation.
   c. Make sure all your verbs are in the past tense.
   d. Make sure your title pages are in the correct format.
2. Work on your PowerPoint.
   a. The focus of your presentation is on Chapters 4 and 5. Summarize the first three chapters; however, talk to your chairperson and ask what precisely he/she wants during this presentation.
   b. Examples of titles of slides can be as follows:
      i. Title
      ii. Statement of the Problem
      iii. Purpose of Study
      iv. Research Questions
      v. Limitations
      vi. Literature Review (quickly summarize significant points)
      vii. Methodology
      viii. Data Collection Procedures
      ix. Research Design
      x. Results (charts and graphs)
      xi. Key Findings (answer your research questions)
      xii. Implications for School Leaders
      xiii. Implications for Further Research
3. Your committee may have a copy of your paper, but you need to provide a copy of the presentation for each member on the day of the defense.
4. Practice, practice, practice! You should know your data results well and communicate what your results mean. Think about possible questions the professors will have about your study. They will drill you on your results and your conclusions.
5. Dress professionally.
6. Be early. Set up the room and double-check your PowerPoint.

7. The professors may ask you to step out of the room before the defense begins to discuss your progress thus far. When you return, you will present.
    a. Expect questions throughout the presentation.
    b. The faculty will make comments about everything and instruct you on revisions you need to make. Do not let this discourage you. View the feedback as assistance to make your final paper the best it can be.
    c. Then, the professors may ask you to leave the room again while discussing your dissertation and deciding if the defense was successful.
    d. When they call you back into the room, have a pen and your paper in front of you. The committee may give critical feedback for you to make corrections before submitting your paper to be published on Proquest or whichever platform your institution uses. Unless the corrections requested are extensive, you may get what you are waiting for: "Congratulations, you have passed your final defense!"

> **SNAPSHOT** 📷
>
> When I arrived at my final defense, one of my co-chairs was not in the room. I was told he would be attending the defense by listening in on his phone. It seemed that he had double-booked his schedule and was preparing for a colonoscopy at the same time. The other committee members kept having to tell him to put his phone on mute. It was funny but also very distracting.

AFTER THE FINAL DEFENSE

- Ask your chair the time frame for revision submission; depending on how close you are to graduation, it is common to have 30 days to make all corrections.
- At this point, you can add your dedication and acknowledgment pages.
- Send the revised dissertation to your committee members and ask for approval to send it to publication (typically Proquest).

ELECTRONIC SUBMISSIONS

Most doctoral theses are posted electronically in Proquest. The doctoral administrative assistant and librarian may offer guidance to you with this process. At this time, you can order a hardbound copy of your work. It is also traditional to give a bound copy to your chairperson or the institution for their support during this process.

THE FINAL DEFENSE

Now you are done.

Congratulations on being a part of a small group of people who have overcome the odds and completed your doctorate. Your perseverance has paid off, and now you can enjoy your accomplishment.

SUMMARY

The dissertation defense focuses on the data, findings, and recommendations of your research and represents a culminating presentation for your doctoral career. This benchmark should only be completed after consulting the dissertation chair. It is also important to verify that the committee has sufficient time to review the document. This chapter has provided important information about the final dissertation defense, a checklist for preparation, and some future steps.

TRAVEL JOURNAL

- What challenges can you anticipate during the final stages of the dissertation defense and publication?
- How will you choose to celebrate your accomplishment?
- What do you plan to do with your anticipated "free" time?

PACKING CHECKLIST

- Plan a way to celebrate your accomplishment. It is okay to party!
- Make your accomplishments known. Post to social media and tag your institution and friends!

Slide titles may include: title page, statement of the problem, research questions, literature review (subtopics with principal studies and researchers), setting, subjects, instruments, limitations of the study, data collection procedures, analysis, findings, conclusions, and recommendations.

Part V

Planning Your Next Adventure

Chapter 12

Career: School Leadership

CHAPTER OBJECTIVES

- Reflect on how your degree aligns with your career goals.
- Identify the job qualification and professional aptitudes you must have to become a district superintendent.
- Identify the job qualification and professional aptitudes you must have to become a district leader.
- Identify the job qualification and professional aptitudes you must have to become a campus principal.
- Explore the options for becoming an educational consultant.

INTRODUCTION

You have spent the last three to four years working on this journey, and now you have reached your final higher education destination; it is time to figure out your next journey. It may seem surreal that you do not have to go to classes anymore, nor do you have to wake up with night sweats, worried about your research. Your and your colleagues' sigh of relief at graduation is real. "Whew, I'm done, and now I am going to take that long-awaited vacation."

Please celebrate and look in the mirror and call yourself Doctor. That euphoria is fleeting. With great titles come significant responsibilities. People have high expectations of people with fancy titles. You are expected to be knowledgeable about the contents of your degree. You are expected to be a competent writer and researcher. You are expected to be articulate and focused on facts, not opinions. You are a scholar!

What are you going to do with this fancy new title?

From the beginning, you were asked to consider the endgame. Your degree and research topic should be the road map of your future professional aspirations. You may have been setting up your career trajectory by networking with fellow students or connecting with influential leaders in your field. Nevertheless, some students get to the finish line and feel lost. They had the dream but are now struggling with how to transition into the real world.

You do have options that you should explore. As we guide new graduates, your path is visible once you look seriously at each avenue of opportunity. You may discover that your dream is initially unrealistic, but something better exists.

MAPPING OUT YOUR FUTURE

What are your options now that you have a doctorate? If you need clarification, seek your university's mentors for their feedback. They may ask you to publish your research in a professional journal where they can be your co-author. They may connect you with people they know in your field to help you network toward your professional goals. Faculty are more than teachers and researchers; the best is still connected to the outside world as consultants. They are actively involved on executive boards or advisory committees and can help you contact the influencers in the field. Focusing on gaining higher-level positions in your current organization is safe, but do not limit yourself. It may be safe, but is it wise?

Exploring new opportunities means not carrying the baggage of your last position. If you were a principal in the district, it does not mean you are the perfect choice as superintendent. You might know too much. Going into a new organization allows you to assess their needs with fresh eyes not clouded by history. Most organizations want new perspectives on their challenges rather than the status quo.

You could embark on a new journey of consulting organizations, especially if they need new perspectives connected to your research. You could also explore the world of higher education. The possibilities are endless, so do not limit your dreams and do something different from what you are doing now. What is the point of all this hard work if you continue to do what you have always done? Be brave.

SCHOOL DISTRICT LEADERSHIP POSITIONS

Superintendent

It is becoming the norm that superintendents should have doctorate degrees. Smaller rural districts may not expect their leader to have a terminal degree, mainly because of budget limitations; however, large urban districts expect people with terminal degrees and are also experienced researchers who know current best practices and can articulate well in speaking and writing. The tenure for district superintendents has fluctuated since COVID-19. The turnover rate has increased to 17.1% in 2022–2023 compared to 16.1% in 2019–2020; 80% of the superintendents who left their positions retired, moved to another position that was not on that level, moved to another state, or died (White, 2023).

Superintendents are expected to have a positive effect on improving student achievement and teacher retention. Waters and Marzano (2007) conducted a meta-analysis of 2,714 school districts across the United States to find the connection between superintendent leadership traits and student achievement. They concluded that five leadership responsibilities that correlated with improved student achievement included:

- The goal-setting process.
- Non-negotiable goals for achievement and instruction.
- Board alignment with and support of district goals.
- Monitor progress on goals for achievement and instruction.
- Use of resources to support the goals for achievement and instruction.

(p. NP)

Superintendents are very visible, and their job is mired in the political culture of their community. They answer only to the school board and are expected to advocate and mediate for the needs of the district's faculty, staff, and students. This job is a 24/7, 365 commitment to the community. Most superintendents have worked up from classroom teacher to campus principal to district leadership positions before attempting to become the definitive leader. Your credibility is based on your leadership record. Whether people have children in your district or not, the whole community wants to know if you are the right person to lead.

Recent years have shown that this position can be plagued by political and social discourse. Knowing how to communicate and promote state initiatives in schools and classrooms is a requirement for the job. When working in a world where a change in educational policies is now the norm, a fundamental sense of adaptability in the culture of the district and state is essential. Not that this has always been the case, but in recent years, rowdy school board meetings due to the hard decisions that had to be made during COVID-19 have highlighted the job's complexity. Curriculum challenges from both ends of the political spectrum have also increased the stress level of these leaders who have put themselves out there for the good of all the children they serve.

It is not a job for the fainthearted. The average tenure of a superintendent is six years (The Broad Center, 2018). Some stay at that pay level to help them achieve the highest retirement pension, but most stay in for many years because they have the heart and soul to make schools a great place for teachers, staff, and children.

The Broad Center (2018) report gave the following reflection questions for anyone seeking the position of superintendent of a school district:

- Do you have a deep understanding of the district's needs, the community's context, and the governing body's expectations?
- Are your skills and experiences a good match for these needs, contexts, and expectations?
- Are you prepared to commit to this district and community long-term to lead the sustainable change they seek?
- Are you focused on leading the district in the time required to meet expectations rather than prioritizing a different long-term plan?
- What are you committed to accomplishing before you seek a career transition?
- Knowing expectations for a superintendent can never be achieved alone, how are you planning to build and sustain a strong team of talented, diverse leaders working with you—inside and outside the system—to provide the support, capacity, and counsel necessary to succeed?
- Do you have personal and professional support systems to rely on during particularly challenging moments?

(p. 15)

The questions are intended to seek applicants fully committed to leading a district to successful academic achievement levels for children. If you are questioning this career path, seek out a current superintendent and ask them for advice. They can give insight into the job and the sacrifices you make personally and professionally if you choose this path. A superintendent can make over $200,000 annually in average-sized districts and close to $500,000 annually in large urban districts. However, as I tell young leaders seeking high leadership positions, you work for every penny of that job. It is not an easy job, and having strong interpersonal and communication skills is essential for success.

DISTRICT-LEVEL LEADERSHIP

Suppose you are seeking leadership positions in curriculum and instruction or human resources. In that case, it is recommended to seek out people already in those positions for perceptions of the actual job duties. Districts are seeking people who have expanded their education to explore new ways of teaching and learning. The need for leaders who can decipher research from vendors pushing the next new trend to save money and time is highly sought. Your level of influence increases with the level of your position. If you want to improve your education, seek these district positions.

You still must be in your field, but now you will see the difference you can make in the lives of the children you support. Starr (2023) describes the roles of district-level leaders as focusing on supporting campus principals, managing state and federal compliance and accountability systems, and strategic communications.

These roles are the buffer between stakeholders and campus operations. District leaders are the solution finders for campus leaders and superintendents and communicate with the community to leverage support for district initiatives.

When considering a district-level leadership position, consider the following reflective questions:

- What strategies do you use to ensure you and your staff remain focused on the school district's mission and vision?
- What is your vision for the future of your department, and what will it look like in your department?
- What are essential qualities you look for when building a high-performing team?
- How do you stay current with curriculum and instruction or human resources trends and innovations and encourage your team to do the same?
- What are the most important lessons in your career, and how have they influenced your leadership style?
- How do you foster a culture of innovation and creativity within your school district?
- What are the biggest challenges facing education today, and what ideas do you have to overcome those challenges?
- What communication style do you use when promoting a change in the district in curriculum and instruction or human resources?

District-level leaders such as directors of curriculum and instruction, operations, or human resources have an average salary between $60,000 and $90,000, depending on the size and location of the school district.

CAMPUS PRINCIPAL

Some leadership doctoral programs lead to principal or superintendent certification. Teachers who seek a doctoral degree tend to go into leadership, and many start their leadership journey in campus leadership positions. Almost all principals start as department chairs, grade level, or assistant principals. These positions are vital in testing how well you manage leadership challenges, such as curriculum and instruction issues and students' academic performance. It expands your sphere of influence as you get higher in the leadership food chain.

Far too many people aspiring to become a principal see the salary as the most significant reason they seek the position, when it needs to be to improve schools for all children. That may sound pretentious, but it is the truth. The job is complex and very demanding.

They say leadership at the top is lonely, and the principal's office can feel very isolated from the rest of the campus community. You answer the teachers, staff, students, parents, district leadership, school board, and community. The evolving role of principals in the past few years has been in campus safety, the emotional and mental support of teachers, and expanding communications with parents and the community (Reid, 2021). Whether you are a secondary, middle, or elementary school principal, the pressure to produce high academic results rests on your shoulders. That said, it is very rewarding if you have the interpersonal skills to relate to all your stakeholders.

Grissom et al. (2021) connected leadership to student learning, not to mention teacher retention.

> Across six rigorous studies estimating principals' effects using panel data, principals' contributions to student achievement were nearly as large as the average effects of teachers identified in similar studies. Principals' effects, however, are larger in scope because they are averaged over all students in a school, rather than a classroom.
>
> (Grissom et al. p. xiv)

The research concluded that campus principals engage in intentional conversations with teachers concerning instruction and data-driven decision-making, build school cultures and climates that foster achievement, facilitate professional learning environments to improve student learning, and manage personnel and resources within their strategic plan for school improvement (p. 58).

If you are considering the option of becoming a campus principal, consider these reflection questions:

- What kind of leader are you? What does this leadership style look like when there is a crisis on campus, such as low student achievement scores, a violent event affecting students, teachers, and staff, or angry parents?
- How do you manage stress during a crisis or conflict?
- Principals should not share confidential information about their faculty or staff, especially if the employee is on a growth plan. How will you manage the situation both personally and professionally?
- How do you feel when you give constructive feedback to an adult?
- What do you know about creating campus improvement plans and monitoring data?
- How do you plan professional development for faculty? How do you plan to monitor whether the instructional strategies are used consistently and with fidelity?
- How comfortable are you in situations where there is conflict? How do you manage conflict?

Campus principal salaries vary depending on the level (secondary or elementary) and the student population attending the school. The range is typically $60,000 to $120,000 if you consider the district location.

EDUCATION CONSULTANT

Consulting is a business and requires a person to be willing to go out and market themselves. If this is your endgame, connecting with organizations is your first job. What can you offer them? What problem must they solve, and what makes you the best person to help them?

Your consulting should be connected to your research agenda. Yes, you finished your research. However, there is more to study. Using the qualitative and quantitative techniques you learned during your degree is essential in consulting. The core of consulting is action research–based. Organizations such as the government and nonprofits want outside perspectives, but they also demand deliverables or solutions. Some nonprofits or education product companies seek consultants to give them the current school perspective for their products or philanthropy. You also may weigh in on the pedological appropriateness of education products. Please note that some states require consultants to get a special license or certification before offering services. Organizations will closely review your credentials and experiences before asking you to step in and advise them. You should be knowledgeable of state and federal regulations. You must know your customer.

Consulting may require setting up your business or limited liability company (LLC). Setting up the business and understanding how taxes and contracts work can protect you from litigation if you do not provide the outcomes the organization expects. You should get some training in creating a business before you begin offering your services as a consultant. Setting up the organizational chart and pay distribution process is also necessary if you have other people in your consulting business.

Becoming a consultant is more complex than offering your knowledge and skills to an organization. It takes planning and a well-thought-out process to find clients, assess their challenges, and realistically state the outcomes you can provide.

- What are the most prominent challenges schools face now, and what can you do to support school districts?
- What is your process for solving problems?
- How do you feel about collaborating with others? Are you open to ideas that are opposed to your belief systems?
- Why do you want to be an advocate for change in the field of education?

- How do you feel about creating your own company with all the legal and financial expectations?

Consultants usually make around $64,000 a year. This salary does not consider the amount of investment you must make to keep your business running.

SUMMARY

There are many options for your future career after obtaining a doctorate. Your path depends on the field you studied and your personal and professional abilities to cope with the challenges within that career choice. There is always an opportunity to change the course of your journey if the career path you start does not fit. Like anything, you will only understand your ability to meet the requirements for a particular position once you are on the job. However, jumping from position to position does not look good on a résumé. Carefully assess your skills and abilities before taking on a position, research the expectations and the organization, and interview others with the same job. Being informed is the best way to find your place and fulfillment in your actions.

TRAVEL JOURNAL

- What is your leadership trajectory? Do you feel comfortable leading people?
- How would you describe your leadership style? How will this style connect with the position you are seeking?
- What is your communication style? Are you comfortable with critical conversations and conflict?
- Are you willing to relocate for a desired position? How would this relocation affect your relationships with your family?

PACKING CHECKLIST

- Shadow a leader who is engaged in the position you are considering as your career goal.
- Research job descriptions of the job you are interested in pursuing.

REFERENCES

Grissom, J. A., Egalite, A. J., & Lindsay, C. A. (2021). *How principals affect students and schools: A systematic synthesis of two decades of research*. The Wallace Foundation. www.wallacefoundation.org/principalsynthesis

Reid, D. B. (2021). US principals' sensemaking of the future roles and responsibilities of school principals. *Educational Management Administration & Leadership, 49*(2), 251–267. https://doi.org/10.1177/1741143219896072

Starr. (2023). On leadership: Rethinking the role of the district curriculum leader. *Phi Delta Kappan, 104*(8), 56–57. https://doi.org/10.1177/00317217231174715

The Broad Center. (2018). *Hire expectations: Big district superintendents stay in their jobs longer than we think*. The Broad Center.

Waters, T. J., & Marzano, R. J. (2007). The primacy of superintendent leadership: The authors' new research finds a strong connection between the work of the district CEO and student achievement. *The School Administrator (Washington), 64*(3), 10.

White, R. S. (2023). Ceilings made of glass and leaving en masse? Examining superintendent gender gaps and turnover over time across the United States. *Educational Researcher*. https://doi.org/10.3102/0013189X231163139

Chapter 13

Career Path: Higher Education

CHAPTER OBJECTIVES

- Discover the different types of universities and their expectations for research and service.
- Analyze how tenure affects faculty promotions.
- Understand the different ranks of faculty at universities.
- Identify key aspects of applying for a faculty job in higher education.

INTRODUCTION

The transition from pre-K–12 to higher education is more significant than most people believe. Education is education. No. There are commonalities, but the structure of the two organizations is as different as cats vs. dogs. Yes, they are both mammals, and the domesticated ones make great pets, but their needs and personalities are entirely different. Pre-K–12 and higher education institutions have similar leadership hierarchies that have boards of trustees on the top. They both must adhere to accreditation criteria to be considered relevant, and they have a curriculum closely aligned with the mission and vision of the fields in which they teach. Furthermore, yes, they have teachers and students.

The differences become apparent when you drill down further. Higher education institutions are geared toward adult learners; therefore, the expectation for students to be independent in their learning is stressed. Students are responsible for getting up in the morning, coming to class, completing their assignments, and fulfilling all the requirements to reach graduation on their own. Faculty usually do not chase students down to come to class or remind them to do their homework. Students in higher education have the choice to do the work or not. It is their dime. Therefore, it is their responsibility. Pre-K–12 institutions and the students' parents closely guide students in each grade level toward completion. At least that is assumed.

CAREER PATH: HIGHER EDUCATION

If your career path is leading you toward higher education, this chapter should help you understand the nuances of the culture and expectations for teaching at this level. There are many benefits to teaching in higher education, like not having to do bus duty or lunch duty, and your work hours are less structured than in pre-K–12. However, you have expectations within each college or university that are above and beyond just teaching. Most universities have work hours that are significantly less structured than in pre-K–12. Depending on the institution or your rank, it could be as many as four to six courses per semester. Faculty may be expected to advise students, serve on school/college or university committees, attend faculty meetings, recruit new students, or work on curriculum.

Most universities require faculty to have structured office hours per week where you are expected to be available for student advising or course support. Whether you teach on campus or online, there are policies on faculty attendance and working for organizations or consulting outside the university.

The faculty are responsible for writing course syllabi, keeping attendance, grading work promptly, and communicating effectively with students and university leadership. Most faculty are hired for 10-month contracts, though some programs are 12 months. If you are on a 10-month contract (fall/spring semesters), it may be possible to teach over the summer months for extra pay. Contracts are usually set up for one year, and faculty evaluations from students and school/college leadership determine whether you will be invited back for another year. Higher ed institutions can vary in contract limitations, so it is essential to ask questions.

CREDENTIALS

Credentials are a combination of your higher education achievements, your certifications or licenses, your research, and your work experience. Before you can teach a particular course, you should have taken at least 18 graduate hours (master's or doctorate) connected to that topic. If you have certification or significant job experience in that area, that helps fulfill the requirements universities must report to the accreditation organizations. You must include your transcripts and curriculum vitae (CV) when sending your application. They will be scrutinized to see if you meet the criteria for teaching the courses they need to be taught. For example, suppose you want to teach graduate-level school leadership courses. In that case, you need to have a doctorate degree in leadership, experience as a school leader, and documentation of publications and presentations for leadership circles.

Only people with doctorate degrees can teach master's and doctoral-level courses. If you want to teach undergraduates, your master's or doctorate should be in the field of study. If the college of education is looking for a professor of early childhood education, they will only call people with a degree and experience in that specific field of study. You cannot teach early childhood methods as a secondary content specialist. As a dean of a college of education, I have had people upset that they did not get an interview. They are often not called because they need the proper credentials for the opening.

UNDERSTANDING THE LANDSCAPE

There are many types of institutions of higher education in the United States. Before you apply for a faculty position, research the type of school where you want to teach.

Some public universities and colleges get financial support from state budgets and federal grants. There are private schools that earn their revenue from donations and student tuition. Some faith-based colleges and universities also get their revenue from student tuition, but their mission is to expand the religion they are affiliated with. Too many applicants for teaching positions need to do their due diligence and research the mission and strategic plan of the university. They make assumptions about their credentials and the expectations of higher education based on their knowledge of pre-K–12 organizations.

The Carnegie Classification of Universities designates universities by level based on research activity and is the guideline for accrediting degree providing institutions (Austin, 2023).

- **Doctoral universities**

Universities >20 research doctoral degrees (not including professional practice)
R1: Highest research activity.
R2: Higher research activity.
R3: Moderate research activity.
Research institutions are ranked based on three indicators:

- The number of research or practice doctorates awarded.
- The amount of money spent on research.
- The number of research faculty.

(Austin, 2023, np)

- **Master's colleges and universities**
- **Baccalaureate colleges**
- **Associate's colleges**
- **Special focus institutions**
- **Tribal colleges**

The level describes the mission and vision of the students who graduate. It also determines what types of people they hire. The more research-oriented the

CAREER PATH: HIGHER EDUCATION

university is, the more likely they hire faculty with detailed research agendas and histories. The systems also guide the process for promotion and tenure. Each level may look different at different universities; however, for the most part, the language is consistent worldwide. The goal is that all faculty strive to move to the next level. Promotion systems and timelines are based on the type of university you are applying to teach.

To simplify the expectations at different levels of universities, the higher the level, the more a professor should focus on research and service. While at baccalaureate colleges, baccalaureate/associate's colleges want faculty to focus more on teaching and service. You need to decide which type of university coincides with your professional goals.

TENURE-TRACK

Tenure can be very controversial in the realm of higher education. "The principal purpose of tenure is to safeguard academic freedom, which is necessary for all who teach and conduct research in higher education" (American Association of University Professors (AAUP), np). Tenure also assures that faculty have a commitment to the university and are more likely to stay for a long time. Who gets tenure

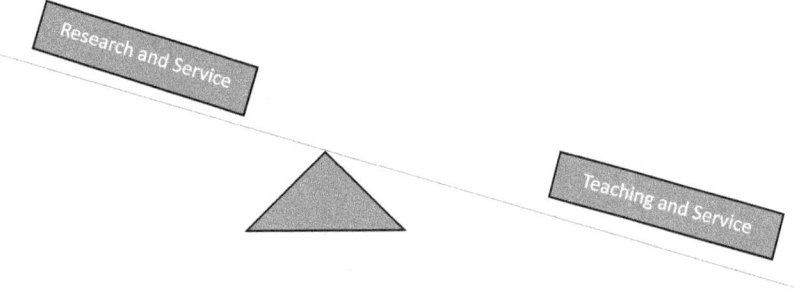

Figure 13.1 R1, R2, R3 university faculty expectations.

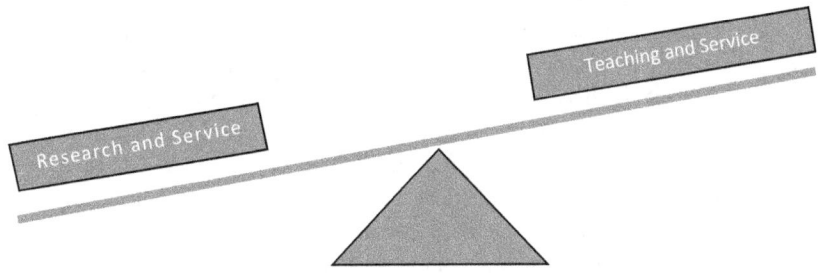

Figure 13.2 Baccalaureate colleges/associate's colleges faculty expectations.

and how the process works varies in each university. Most universities are faculty-governed, and the tenure requirements are within their power and control. These universities allow faculty to determine the policies for promotion and tenure.

> **SNAPSHOT** 📷
>
> One of the basic principles of university life is "faculty governance," which means that decisions involving the mission of the university properly rest with the faculty. So it's conceivable that the faculty members of a unit (department, college, etc.) would formulate criteria for obtaining tenure that excludes research and writing (i.e., tenure could be awarded based solely on a candidate's teaching, service, consulting, or other activities). It was rare, but I did encounter such criteria when I served on a university-level promotion and tenure committee.

Tenure-track faculty are required to document teaching, research, and service performance. Annual evaluations review the extent to which a faculty member exhibits a scholar's attributes—teaching evaluations center on student reviews and annual evaluations. Research expectations focus on how many peers reviewed articles, books, and presentations the faculty member publishes during an academic year. Tenure-track faculty must serve both in the university and the community by participating, leading committees, or serving on advisory boards for outside organizations. Depending on the university, a faculty member can qualify for tenure after they achieve the associate professor rank. To qualify for tenure or promotion of rank, a faculty member must have extensive documentation of their teaching, research, and service. This big binder of documentation (yes, many universities still require binders) and recommendations is submitted to a promotion committee, which gives recommendations to senior leaders of the university for approval.

It is a goal for many faculty members in higher education to get promoted and receive tenure. Tenured professors have job security in many universities, unless they break the law, there is a financial crisis at the university, or the tenured professor's research grant is discontinued. The history of tenure is centered on academic freedom and goes back hundreds of years. Academia needs to explore phenomenon and theories in context of the current worldview. Those views are not always popular with the public at large and can be controversial. Tenure gives faculty safeguards to protect their academic freedom. Thus, tenure was created. There are opponents of tenure systems. There are many lawsuits against universities by professors who did not qualify for tenure and believe they did not qualify due to a system that discriminates against minorities and women. State legislators have been promoting the dismantling of tenure in state schools due to the controversial discussions surrounding race, gender, and economic disparities (Stewart, 2022). The process for getting tenure takes years. A faculty member must show a consistent, long-term commitment to the foundations of academia. There may be a boost in salary at every level of promotion, but that is not a guarantee.

NON-TENURE-TRACK

Faculty not teaching in a research-specific field are usually considered non-tenure-track. Non-tenure-track faculty must excel in teaching and service. They can still be promoted in rank but only qualify for tenure with the research component. Some teaching universities are not research institutions that will give tenure-tracks to non-research faculty. "Publish or perish" is still a reality in many research-focused universities, so be aware of this requirement before applying for teaching positions. You may enter higher education as a second career, and moving up the ranks of academia is not a priority; you may be happy to stay as an instructor or assistant professor. To expand their research, professors will actively seek grant money to fund their research and to buy equipment. If you are interested in tenure-track, you can begin building your publication database by submitting papers that you are writing in your doctoral classes. Talk to your faculty about sponsoring your submissions to publications. After you are finished with your dissertation, you can publish a condensed version that summarizes your study and results.

FACULTY RANK

Faculty rank is the pecking order in the university. Your rank determines what kind of office you get, what classes you can choose to teach, and even whether you get your first choice of a new laptop. Pay raises are also associated with rank, though it varies per university. All in all, rank is significant in the halls of academia. New faculty who does not have higher education teaching experience are hired at a low rank, such as instructors, lecturer, or assistant professor. If you are planning to make higher education your career path, you will be working to build your CV with presentations, publications, and university service. Following is a figure that shows the different faculty ranks at most universities. Each university has a policy of how long someone must be at a rank before they can apply for a promotion. Before applying for promotion, three to four years of higher education experience as an assistant professor are common.

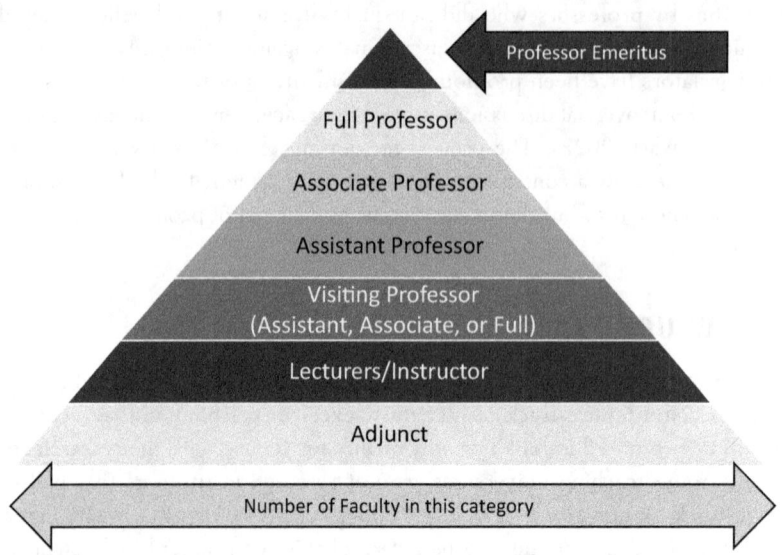

Figure 13.3 Ranks of faculty in relation to number of faculty.

ADJUNCTS

Adjuncts are part-time employees who teach classes on all levels, undergraduate to doctoral. They must be credentialed to teach the courses they are assigned to teach before they can be hired. Adjuncts are not offered benefits. They are hired when they are needed. If a full-time faculty member's course does not have the required number of students and is closed, a full-time faculty member can "bump" an adjunct and take their course. Full-time faculty must have the number of courses required in their contract; adjuncts do not have that requirement. Most university policy handbooks limit the number of courses an adjunct teaches. It would be best to ask how many courses you can teach per semester. Adjuncts usually do not create a new syllabus for a course but use the syllabus approved by the college or school. Online adjuncts usually teach predeveloped courses and have no say in the sequence of topics or assignments. Accreditation organizations require consistency in terms of curriculum across all classes.

This limitation of changes in the curriculum means an adjunct cannot pick the textbook and assignments. This policy keeps adjuncts from teaching from their agenda on the topic instead of sticking to the set curriculum of the field. There have been instances where an adjunct goes on an unapproved tangent of topics and puts students at risk of being unprepared to take certification exams or unprepared for the next course in the sequence.

Adjunct faculty are paid by the course, and that pay varies depending on the university. Adjuncts are not usually given a computer, nor do they have an office to work in during the day. The time the courses are offered is not based on the adjunct's availability, that is, if they cannot teach an 8:00 a.m. class, then they will not teach that class. The course schedule is created months before the semester begins, and adjuncts are assigned after all full-time faculty have received their course assignments. Adjuncts are the last hired for teaching jobs.

Adjuncts are evaluated, so expect an observation by the department chair or designated faculty member. End-of-course evaluations completed by students are weighed heavily in the review process. Adjuncts must abide by all deadlines for grades and be available for office hours if students in the class need extra help. Reliable adjuncts who have good student reviews could be considered for a full-time position. Adjuncts are relatively inexpensive employees, so many universities are using more and more adjuncts to save money.

LECTURERS/INSTRUCTORS

Lecturers and instructors are very similar titles, but each level's pay may differ. These faculty members are usually full-time and teach specialized courses in a field. If someone does not have a terminal degree but they have all the other credentials to teach, the university may hire them as a lecturer or instructor for undergraduate students. Some faculty members do not want to do what is required for the tenure-track, so this level rank does not expect extra work. However, some lecturers/instructors want to work their way into the tenure-track and qualify to become assistant professors. This position is full-time with benefits, but the pay is typically low. The average salary for lecturers/instructors varies depending on the tier of the university. The average is $50,000 per year.

VISITING FACULTY

Visiting faculty come from other universities to teach or research for a short period of time. They usually hold a tenured position at another university and visit others to share their expertise with a wider audience. These faculty members could be anything from assistant to full professors and are treated at their host campus like any other faculty member. They still must do the instructional duties of writing syllabi, grading papers, and submitting grades. Their salary is dependent upon their rank and the field of expertise.

ASSISTANT PROFESSOR

Assistant professors are often referred to as junior faculty. This rank is the first level of faculty who may be seeking tenure. Most new full-time faculty come in at this level. If you are a new graduate and have already been an adjunct or lecturer/instructor, you will probably enter the university system as an assistant professor.

The goal for most junior faculty is to build their academic portfolio to be promoted to associate professor. This process includes actively seeking committee memberships, presenting at conferences, publishing articles, and providing high-quality instruction to students.

Promotion committees appreciate it when faculty go above and beyond and make themselves known beyond the school/college they are assigned. Getting involved in campus-wide events and showing interest in the faculty senate or other committees is essential. One faculty member who wanted exposure to the promotion/tenure committee volunteered to be the name-caller at graduation. She attended all the registration events and networked with leaders and staff. Her dean supported her by sharing her publications and presentations with the campus newsletter and highlighting her work with students. She was promoted! This process for moving up in higher ed is about building relationships and earning a good reputation with the other faculty and leadership. The average pay, depending on the tier of the university, is $60,000.

ASSOCIATE PROFESSOR

The next level is an associate professor. To achieve this promotion, an assistant professor should demonstrate competence in at least two areas: research, teaching, and service. The associate professors who want to qualify for a full professorship must add leadership activities to their portfolios. They should be striving to be program coordinators or department chairs. These leadership positions, research, teaching, and service qualify them for applying to full professor. The average pay, depending on the tier of the university, is $65,000.

FULL PROFESSOR

A full professor is the only ranking faculty member called a "professor." Nothing disturbs a full professor more than someone referring to an assistant, an associate, or my goodness, an adjunct as a professor. These faculty members worked very hard to achieve this rank and status. The benefits of this rank mean they get first choice of courses, can give significant input on times and days of classes, have premiere office space, and in some colleges where parking is a premium, a parking space! It would be best to refer to yourself as a professor only if you are a full professor.

Being specific on your title is especially true of your email signature. Some, not all, full professors expect you to call them "doctor" and not by their first name. This status is nothing to take lightly, even though you had a prestigious position in the pre-K education world. If you were a superintendent who moved to higher education, you must remember to start at the bottom of the pecking order. Some school leaders struggle with this transition, so walk in humbly and accept your new status. Full professors in education can earn anywhere from $80,000 to $100,000, depending on the university.

PROFESSOR EMERITUS

Professor emeritus status is awarded to outstanding professors who retire after many years of service. A professor of this status has been a full-tenured professor for over ten years and has a reputation for outstanding teaching and research.

They are allowed to continue to teach at the university if they choose. Most of these professors are over 65 years old and usually come back to lecture or give seminars. They can keep their full salary and benefits as they work primarily part-time. For a professor to qualify for emeritus status, they are recommended by other professors or leaders, undergo an interview process, and are approved by the university's board of directors. They are celebrated at end-of-year faculty celebrations and sometimes at graduations.

FINDING A JOB AT A HIGHER EDUCATION INSTITUTION

The Search

When looking for a teaching position at a higher education institution, you should focus on the ones that fit your teaching and scholarship goals. Review the university tier system chart and determine what is the right choice for you. Tiers I and III will only consider your application if you have extensive research history beyond your dissertation. There are job search sites like HigherEdJobs.com and BlacksinHigherEd.com. Both sites will guide you in creating a profile, and you will upload your CV. If you want to teach at a local university, you must check their website often. Positions open up all year, not just in the spring. The adjunct applications are open all the time. Colleges of education try to create a pool of adjuncts to access what they need without delay. If a faculty member gets sick or must quit, an adjunct may be called to fill in for the rest of the semester.

When looking for a position, read the job requirements and expectations closely. If they are looking for someone to teach secondary math and you have a secondary English degree, do not apply. If they are looking for doctoral faculty, only apply if you have experience working on a dissertation committee or extensive research in that doctorate. A medical doctor once applied for a professor position in the education leadership doctoral program. He had no educational experience, only medical. He was not called for an interview. Only expect people to call you once you apply if they want to interview you.

The department chairs get many applications and weed out those that do not fit the qualifications. They do not have time to call each applicant and say why they did not choose them. Please refrain from calling the dean or president of the university to promote yourself for a position. Some applicants call or email senior leaders for a tour and meeting to get their foot in the door. Most deans and presidents allow the search committee to review applicants and try to avoid influencing the process.

The Application

When filling out the online application, spell every word correctly and give accurate information. If you do not answer a question on the application, your application may not go forward. Be honest. If you have a criminal record, a background check will expose you. If you are applying for a faith-based school, you may be asked to share the name of your church and pastor and list how you volunteer there. Have your transcripts and recommendation letters ready to upload. If you only have unofficial transcripts, that is fine until you are called for a formal interview. Request official transcripts to be sent to the university once you are invited to an interview.

The Interviews

The interview process for a faculty member position is very intense. An applicant is only invited to campus if they are one of the finalists. Only go to campus if you are comfortable with the salary. A budget line was set for this position, and little wiggle room exists. An applicant came to the university for an interview.

There are multiple interviews for a position in most universities. You may have a screening interview online with the search committee; if you are a finalist and your credentials, background, and reference checks work out, you might be invited to campus. There you will interview the search committee and department chair. In small universities, you may meet with upper-level leaders, but not in large universities.

You may be asked to give a teaching demonstration and possibly a research presentation to discuss your research history and agenda. The teaching demonstration will be presented to the college/school faculty. If this is a requirement for the position, you will be asked to teach a lesson in your field. This presentation should take at most 30 minutes, but ask the search committee chair about their expectations. The audience will give feedback from the teaching demonstration and research presentation to the search committee. Your lesson should reflect how you will teach the students for whom you are being hired. If you are applying to teach elementary science methods courses, then you will demonstrate how you will teach a lesson to undergraduate education majors. The more hands-on and the less you lecture, the better. Your slideshow should be creative and concise—spelling and grammar count. Using technology such as a video, game, or survey will only benefit the impression you give.

The search committee hopes to get to know you better between presentations. They want to ensure your personality will be an asset to their college/

school. The interviews will lead to a recommendation or non-recommendation. If the applicant is recommended, the president will recommend him/her to the board of trustees for final approval. The approval may take a few days, so do not panic if you do not hear anything the next day. There are a lot of moving parts. You will probably get a contract through email, and once you sign it, you are hired!

Curriculum Vitae vs. Résumé

A curriculum vitae, required for university-level positions, and a résumé are very different documents. A *résumé* is a two- to three-page document about your work history, university degrees, and certifications. Résumés also include job objectives and bullet points of teaching and leadership qualities. A curriculum vitae (CV) is a much longer and more detailed description of everything you have done in your career. These documents can be much longer than most people coming into higher education are familiar with.

The following are some examples of the subtitles on a CV:

- Name with degree level: "Dr. John Smith" or "John Smith, PhD." Do not put "Dr. John Smith, EdD."
- Contact information: email address, address, phone number.
- Education history: most recent degree to undergraduate degree, year of graduation, and title of dissertation or thesis.
- Certification: all certifications, including state and training credentials.
- Higher education teaching experience: group each higher education institution in order from most recent to past teaching experiences.
  - Faculty rank (adjunct, assistant professor, etc.)
  - Courses taught. Include the name of the university, year, subject taught, list of all courses taught, including level (UG, grad, doctoral), course rubric (EDUC 900), and course title. Delineate whether the course was taught online, in person, or hybrid. You can add student evaluation scores to show that your students like you!
  - If you created an online course—year, level, rubric, and title.
  - Committees or service at the university.
- Other work experience: this is where you document your professional experience, including leadership and teaching roles.
- Publications.
- Presentations.
- Grants or fellowships.
- Professional Organizations: note if you have a leadership role.
- Community service.
- References upon request.

Writing a CV takes some time since you need to go back and find all the documentation of trainings you have attended and given, and certificates and certifications with expiration dates. Some universities post faculty CVs online, which are shared with promotion committees. Once it is organized, it is easy to update with courses, presentations, and publications. Do not add pictures of yourself. The paper should be white and have no fancy font.

Your CV is a culmination of all your work in your career that has led you to this point. It is exciting to begin a new adventure. If the pay is too much of a disappointment now, keep working in your current place until you retire.

SUMMARY

Teaching in higher education may seem easy, but it is very complicated and riddled with policies and expectations.

If you want to learn more about teaching at this level, meet with your university advisor or research chairperson to learn more about the job. Learning as much as possible before abandoning a career you love is always a good idea. Accept the possibility that you may have to relocate to work at a university that meets your criteria. There are so many great things about working at a university, especially if you are training future teachers. It gives you such hope for the future of our profession to see such bright and excited people wanting to change the world. Your influence could make an impact on future generations of schoolchildren. What could be better?

TRAVEL JOURNAL

- Consider your best and worst higher ed faculty members that taught classes during your college experience. What did they do and not do that made you remember them?
- How will you use your personal experience as a student to guide you as a teacher of adult learners?
- What do you perceive your daily schedule will look like if you become a faculty member at a university? Share this perception with a university mentor to determine if this is really the case.
- How are you preparing yourself for the change in salary if you are moving from pre-K–12 to higher education?

> **PACKING CHECKLIST**
> - Research higher education job sites for open positions that fit your qualifications.
> - Create a curriculum vitae.
> - Read the university websites very carefully to understand their mission and vision statements.
> - Apply for positions only if your qualifications meet the standards set in the job posting.

REFERENCES

American Association of University Professors. (n.d.). *Recommended institutional regulations on academic freedom and tenure*. Retrieved June 30, 2023, from www.aaup.org/report/recommended-institutional-regulations-academic-freedom-and-tenure

Austin, S. L. (2023). *Carnegie classifications, college tiers, and what they mean*. https://academicinfluence.com/resources/guidance/carnegie-classifications-college-tiers

Stewart, M. (2022). *Tenure under attack. Insight into diversity*. Retrieved June 30, 2023, from www.insightintodiversity.com/tenure-under-attack/

Bon Voyage

It is a strange feeling when this process is finished. As you reflect on all the days you spent writing, attending classes, and being in meetings with your faculty members, I hope you can see why this journey was challenging but also necessary. If it were easy, you would not enjoy the success at the end quite as much. It is like all challenges you take on; if anyone could do it, why bother? Take what you have learned and be the leader that influences change in our complex world. It will be surreal when people call you Doctor and look at you like you have all the answers. In truth, you have not become the all-knowing academic with a fancy new title in the room. You become someone who now knows how to seek answers from your fellow researchers in the club you have joined. You are just beginning a lifetime of learning and sharing what you know with those who look to you for guidance and support. Lead well, my friends.

Index

10-year rule 23

ABD (All But Dissertation) 9, 64, 77
abstract 35, 42, 95, 107, 112, 115
academic integrity 72
academic reading 29, 42
academic reading skills 29
academic writing 29, 41, 45, 62, 72
academic writing skills 29, 45, 62; *see also* academic writing
accommodations 44, 45
accreditation organizations 15, 16, 25, 131, 136
Accrediting Commission for Community and Junior Colleges (ACCJC) 15
action research 63, 127
activist 35
adjuncts 5, 86, 136, 137, 138, 139, 141
adult learning theory 29, 30, 31, 32, 36, 130, 142
andragogy 30, 31
APA style 40, 41, 71, 99
application 8, 11, 30, 34, 36, 103, 104, 131, 139, 140
artificial intelligence (AI) 67, 71, 72
assignments 16, 21, 22, 29, 32, 37, 39, 40, 44, 45, 47, 50, 51, 52, 54, 56, 59, 60, 61, 62, 65, 67, 68, 69, 72, 73, 86, 90, 96, 130, 136, 137

assistant professor 135, 137, 138, 141
associate professor 86, 134, 138
attendance 59, 68, 88, 131

Bandura 37, 38
bias research 80, 81
bibliography 98, 99
Blackboard 21, 51, 68, 69
Blooms Taxonomy 34

campus based 15, 16, 17, 20, 23, 24
campus principal 121, 123, 124, 125, 126, 127
Canvas 21, 68, 69
capstone projects 59, 62, 63, 64, 65, 70
career goals 77, 121, 128
The Carnegie Classification of Universities 132
Carnegie Hours 50
The Carnegie Project on the Education Doctorate (CPED) Resource Center 63
The Carnegie Unit 50
The College Board's Scholarship 11
chairperson 6, 64, 84, 86, 87, 88, 89, 93, 100, 101, 103, 104, 111, 112, 113, 114, 115, 116, 141
cohort programs 7, 8
cohort systems 23
committee chair *see* chairperson

INDEX

committee members 6, 18, 38, 64, 65, 86, 88, 92, 93, 104, 111, 112, 115, 116, 138
complaints about faculty 70
comprehensive exams 17, 39, 59, 62, 64, 65, 66, 70, 112
continuous enrollment 67, 70
coping strategies 54, 55, 72
Council of Graduate Schools 7
counterarguments 106
credentials 15, 16, 127, 131, 132, 136, 137, 140, 141
critical reading skills 42
curriculum vitae (CV) 15, 86, 131, 135, 139, 141, 142, 143

data analysis 101, 105
data collection 94, 97, 101, 111, 112, 115, 117
deadlines and timeframes 111, 112
definition of terms 97
department chair 23, 70, 88, 125, 137, 138, 139, 140
discussion of results (interpretations) 105
dissertation defense 112, 114, 115, 117
Dissertation in Practice (DiP) 63, 65, 70, 86, 96
district leader 14, 71, 121, 122, 123, 125, 126

Ed.D. 6, 7, 8, 13, 14, 48, 63, 141
education consultant 127
education specialist 7
electronic submissions 116

faculty rank 86, 135, 141
Fast Web 11
final defense 11, 42, 88, 112, 114, 115, 116
financial aid 11, 69
formal tone 40
Free Application for Federal Student Aid (FAFSA) 11
full professor 137, 138, 139

generalizations 107
graduate GPA 5
Graduate Record Exam (GRE) 5
graduation rates 16, 78, 81
graduation regalia 12

Higher Learning Commission (HLC) 15

Implications for Further Research 106, 115
implications for leaders 106
Institutional Review Boards (IRBs) and Protection of Human Subjects 103
instruments 93, 94, 96, 101, 102, 104, 111, 112, 117
interviews 5, 68, 79, 80, 96, 100, 101, 102, 104, 106, 128, 132, 139, 140, 141
IRB approval 11, 38, 79, 102, 105, 112

Kolb's theory of learning styles 35

learning cycle 35
learning style 3, 14, 21, 24, 29, 35, 36, 45, 52
lecturers and instructors 137
limitations 20, 22, 35, 97, 98, 103, 111, 112, 115, 117, 122, 131, 136
literature review 39, 42, 43, 60, 97, 98, 99, 109, 111, 112, 115, 117
logical fallacies 107

methodology 42, 43, 60, 100, 115
Middle States Commission on Higher Education (MSCHE) 15
mixed methods 97, 100, 101
mixed strategy 61
motivation 3, 30, 34, 35, 37, 38

natural language processing (NLP) 72
New England Commission of Higher Education (NECHE) 15
Non Tenured Track 135

INDEX

Northwest Commission on Colleges and Universities (NWCCU) 15
NVIDIA 72

online 7, 11, 12, 14, 15, 17, 19, 20, 21, 22, 23, 24, 36, 37, 40, 41, 45, 50, 69, 71, 90, 98, 99, 100, 102, 103, 131, 136, 140, 141, 142
online courses 19, 20, 37, 141
organizational skills 29, 39

participants *see* subjects
pedagogy 30, 35
Ph.D. 6, 8, 13, 14, 64, 141
plagiarism 43, 67, 68, 71, 72, 92
planners 61
pragmatist 35, 36
preproposal/ candidacy defense 88, 111, 112
procedures 3, 4, 24, 59, 63, 100, 101, 102, 104, 111, 112, 115, 117
professor emeritus 139
proposal defense 95, 103, 104, 111
The Publication Manual of the American Psychological Association or APA Manual 40
Purdue Owl 41
purpose of the study 96

qualitative 43, 82, 84, 88, 97, 100, 101, 104, 127
quantitative methodology 43, 100, 101

recommendation letters 140
recommendations 12, 53, 64, 65, 70, 80, 82, 106, 112, 114, 117, 134, 140, 141
reference page 99, 109
reflector 35
reliability 88, 93, 102, 105
research articles 22, 39, 42, 47, 98, 100, 109
research design 60, 88, 97, 100, 101, 115

research questions 80, 94, 96, 97, 101, 102, 104, 105, 111, 112, 115, 117
resume 87, 128, 141
revisers 61

Sallie Mae's database 11
scholarly writing 40
scholarships 11, 13, 69, 139
Section 504 of the Rehabilitation Act of 1973 44
self-care 54
self-efficacy 37, 38, 43
setting 7, 12, 17, 20, 29, 43, 44, 61, 86, 101, 111, 112, 117, 121, 127
Southern Association of Colleges and Schools Commission on Colleges (SACSCOC) 15
statistics 29, 43, 51, 100
subjects 77, 78, 80, 87, 101, 103, 104, 112, 117, 141
superintendent 12, 14, 78, 83, 88, 101, 121, 122, 123, 124, 125, 138
syllabus 21, 37, 51, 67, 68, 69, 136

technology 7, 21, 22, 24, 38, 72, 78, 101, 140
tenure 122, 123, 130, 133, 134, 135, 137, 138
tenured professors 86, 134
tenure-track 14, 133, 134, 135, 137
terminal degree 6, 7, 8, 9, 82, 122, 137
theoretical framework 95, 96, 105, 106
theorist 30, 35, 36
time management 39, 48, 50, 52, 56, 64, 108
topic of research 79
traditional dissertation 63, 64
transfer credits 7, 23, 25
transferring master's degree hours 23
tuition 9, 11, 52, 64, 67, 69, 70, 132

147

upside-down pyramid or funnel 80
U.S. Census Bureau 6

validity 62, 88, 93, 96, 97, 102, 105
VARK 35
visiting faculty 137

WASC Senior College and
    University Commission
    (WSCUC) 15
Western Association of Schools and
    Colleges 15
Work Area and Supplies 53, 54